Simon French

CANNILY, CANNILY

PUFFIN BOOKS

Published with the assistance of the Literature Board
of the Australia Council.

All characters and places in this book are wholly fictitious,
and any resemblance to any person living or dead is coincidental.

Puffin Books, Penguin Books Ltd, Harmondsworth, Middlesex, England
Penguin Books, 40 West 23rd Street, New York, New York 10010, U.S.A.
Penguin Books Australia Ltd, Ringwood, Victoria, Australia
Penguin Books Canada Ltd, 2801 John Street, Markham, Ontario, Canada L3R 1B4
Penguin Books (N.Z.) Ltd, 182–190 Wairau Road, Auckland 10, New Zealand

First published by Angus & Robertson Publishers, Australia, 1981
First published in Great Britain by Angus & Robertson (U K) Ltd
Published in Puffin Books 1983

Copyright © Simon French, 1981
All rights reserved

Made and printed in Great Britain by Cox & Wyman, Ltd, Reading
Filmset in Monophoto Times by Northumberland Press Ltd, Gateshead

For Trevor

Contents

Yesterday

Once there had been a beach.

He could hear the waves pounding on the shore, feel the sand between his toes; he could see himself running into the water. He thought about it often.

Back then he had been much younger, a small child not yet at school, but memories were stubborn sorts of things. Waves, sand and water were mixed up with other recollections – good night kisses and stories read aloud, being afraid of the dark. It seemed so long ago sometimes, but he would often dream about it all, waking up expecting the beach to be real.

But they had moved away. The coast had been left for places further inland, for the infinite stretches of bushland, plains and country towns.

He could see a road now, a deep grey stripe in the midst of a formless landscape. Things came into focus gradually: trees appeared, yellow paddocks, misted green hills and on the road, the green and white Kombivan. Closer and closer it came, until he could see in detail the luggage and spare tyres on the roof rack, the dent in the back mudguard, the broken foglight, the caravan in tow. And it all moved slowly, relentlessly over the landscape along the endless road into dusk.

They were moving again. Somewhere behind was a cold southern township where they had stayed for three months. Its memory was already insignificant, its images of place and people blurred. Most distinct was the school, where he'd sat in a brick classroom, in one corner with all the other fruitpickers' kids. But they were moving to another town now, further to the north. It was like this all the time and with bemused resignation he guessed that the next place would be much the same as the last.

He felt very tired. They had been driving for a long time now, and he began to long for sleep, for peace and quiet.

The Kombi's interior was alive with noise, because every corner of the van rattled. The wind whistled in through a dozen unseen cavities, the loose doors sounded like an orchestra of castanets and above all this was the unending cough-splutter of the engine – a penetrating undercurrent of sound that changed pitch with each change of gears.

He lay awake on the makeshift bunk in the back of the Kombi, wedged between built-in cupboards and boxes of belongings. Gusts of night air brushed against his exposed face as the rest of him huddled warm inside the sleeping bag, and in the distance of the front seat he could see his parents. His mother was curled up asleep, shrouded in blankets, her calm face silhouetted against the dark. And fleetingly, he could see his father's bearded face reflected in the rear view mirror.

'You awake, Trevor?'

'Yeah. Kind of.'

'You hungry?'

'No. Will we be there soon?'

'Few more hours. Try and get some sleep, eh?'

They drove on into the night.

The dashboard lights glowed against the shadows, flickering like the dials of a strange machine. The headlights shone into the mysterious distance, hypnotically revealing an infinite road . . . slowly, very slowly, Trevor drifted into sleep.

When at last the Kombi and caravan stopped for the final time that night he awoke, and guessed that they had arrived.

Two

'I'm going to be a bricklayer.'

He snapped back into the present. 'A what?'

'A bricklayer,' said his father with a grin. 'You know . . .'

'You've never done that before.'

'Yes I have. A long time ago, when you were little.'

'Oh.'

Sometimes his parents were an enigma to him, a past beyond clear memory. In his mind he could picture them working among monotonous, endless rows of fruit trees. Before that there were only vague and disjointed images of a place that had come before the seasonal work they now followed.

'The money's good,' Buckley said with his usual reassuring optimism.

'But how come you're doing bricklaying now, Dad?'

'A change is as good as a holiday.'

So they had arrived.

Trevor hated caravan parks.

He disliked the temporary, disorganized life, the clutter of caravans and cars and people's possessions, the dust in summer, the mud in wet weather.

Home, he thought grimly. Funny sort of home, a caravan and a Kombi with a tent annexe to connect the two. The caravan was small and incredibly cramped. Cupboards in every conceivable place, a double bunk for his parents, a small gas stove, a fridge, a pint-sized table and chairs for meals, a portable TV sitting on the floor. He always marvelled at the wealth of belongings that came to light each time they unpacked – books, records, guitars, a harmonica. There were photo albums too, and an old surfboard that seemed to be permanently lashed to the Kombi's roof rack because Buckley couldn't bear to part with it.

The Kombivan was Trevor's bedroom, a very makeshift affair. Pictures of soccer teams and pop bands on the walls and ceiling, eleven years' worth of toys and possessions crammed into the cupboards under his bunk, all his clothes in the old tea chest behind the driver's seat.

Home. The caravan park seemed empty of other people, a garish plot of land that perched uncomfortably against the backdrop of country township and rural countryside. There was a cluster of onsite caravans nearby and around these the caravan park sprawled, barren, untidy, and held together by the lengths of coloured lights strung between the boundary trees.

'I don't like it here much.'

'Give it time, Trevor,' his mother said. 'You've barely been here a day.'

'I know that, but . . .'

When the weather was warm like this she wore bleached calico or floral cotton dresses that swept about her ankles and often-bare feet. He liked her quietness and her understanding and often thought how strange it seemed, her living in a caravan.

'What are you going to do, though? There's no fruit to pick.'

She was in the caravan, sorting through cupboards of clothing. 'Seem to have accumulated some things that need washing here,' she said absently, then looked at him and raised her eyebrows. 'Oh, I'm not going to work, if that's

13

what you mean. I think it's time for a break. Your dad seems to be bounding with energy, though.'

'So how long are we gonna be here?'

'Anything up to six months. Building extensions at a bowling club, or something. I still haven't heard the full story.'

'But what are you going to be doing?' he asked again, not persistently but out of interest. 'All that time?'

She shrugged. 'Sew. Make things. Read books. Get bored.'

Sometimes a sign would be taped to the caravan's window: 'Dressmaker', in flowing textawritten letters. This time it hadn't appeared, because Kath was only able to make money out of it in the larger towns and the more popular caravan parks. But every so often, when the sign was up, she would sit at the sewing machine in the caravan making clothes. It made a change from fruitpicking, but depended on a lot of things – her mood, the weather, the money situation.

With the sign for advertising, she made things – shirts, skirts and dresses for tourists and tourists' children. And sometimes there'd be things for Trevor – shirts, trousers and the patchwork shoulderbag he took to school.

The town lay huddled and largely forgotten by the outside world. It looked like many other country townships, with its tranquil and orderly streets of old weatherboard houses, its small quota of churches and haphazard cemeteries. Once, it must have been an important place – the monumental School of Arts building testified to some sort of past glory. Now there was only the necessary colour of the musty shops and obligatory supermarket to define much of what was left. There were also the trees along the main street, lofty Norfolk pines planted decades before to commemorate the same wars the memorial in the neglected park did.

14

Behind the town, along the fringes of bushland, the timber mill laboured on as it had done for many years. Amid its complex of open sheds and timber-stacked yard, the conical incinerator rose up like a black pyramid, feeding on scrap wood and sawdust, sending a continual drift of blue-grey smoke into the sky. The mill was the town's only industry and many of the locals worked there, operating the screaming saws, stacking cut timber in the yard, loading up the semi-trailers with telegraph poles and building beams.

Around all this, bushy hills and open countryside stretched into the horizon.

The highway bypassed the town by some distance, and only a token trickle of tourists made the effort to leave the main road. When they arrived in the town they did so noisily in shiny cars and gaudy, impractical four-wheel-drives. They took photos, bought petrol at the two-pump petrol station, downed drinks and food at the R.S.L. Club or the Lindsay Hotel, and then they left.

The people who lived there were few and unchanging. Those who lived along the orderly streets had probably done so all their lives, in houses their grandparents had built. Others lived on outlying farms and came into town maybe once a week for shopping and supplies. The men were stern, practical country people who wore riding boots and Akubra hats and talked about crops and stock. Together with the people who lived and worked in the town, they and their wives benevolently regarded the tourists as misguided city fools, and treated change with suspicion. The caravan park at the edge of town was the most recent gesture made to change and tourism, but it was unsuccessful. The few tourists only stayed overnight, and so the single men who worked at the timber mill filled the onsite caravans.

They were in the supermarket.

15

Methodically, Kath and Buckley explored the aisles, alternately grabbing items from the grocery shelves and referring to a hastily scribbled shopping list.

'Butter?'

'Yes.'

'Eggs?'

'Yes.'

'Tea milk bread orange juice soap mosquito coils?'

'Got them.'

Trevor ambled unenthusiastically behind, pushing the shopping trolley. Shopping wasn't interesting him very much and he found himself instead taking note of the other people in the supermarket. It was a Saturday morning, busy and crowded. There were townspeople, farmers and their rural wives with their windblown, expressionless faces, skinny, freckled kids. At a distance, Trevor played silent games with these strangers, allocating each one an occupation and a personality. The people who noticed him watching them returned his apparent curiosity with their own inquisitive looks. It was like being in a foreign country, he decided.

'We need the trolley, Trevor. Can you hurry up?'

'Okay, okay.'

He was gazing into the glass doors of the dairy products refrigerator. In the background of the reflection were the vaguely mirrored figures of his parents. Buckley he could see quite clearly – short and stocky, wide-eyed and casual, a face defined by tousled ginger hair and a straggly beard. Kath's reflection was less solid, because she kept moving around. But he caught glimpses of her face, thin and girlishly plain, and her long plaited hair, almost the same colour as Buckley's.

Trevor started to think, *sometimes she looks like a schoolgirl*, and then stopped short, because he could see his father pulling faces at him.

16

'Wakey, wakey, Trev. We need the trolley here, not half a mile away.'

'All right, I'm coming.'

'You're so slow today. What's wrong?'

'Just tired, I guess.'

At that moment, he had started thinking about school. It was a depressing prospect and an unknown quantity that lurked on the horizon of the Monday to come. He finally decided that it'd probably be like any of the other country schools he had been to, but even that comparison left him feeling uncomfortable. He started to wonder what the other kids in this town would be like.

As they were leaving the supermarket, Kath gave him a bag of groceries to carry back to the Kombi. Outside, there was the usual Saturday morning activity about the place – the other people shopping, clusters of dusty cars and utilities almost filling the width of the main street. Holding the bag of groceries in one arm, Trevor strolled along the footpath, glancing indifferently into shop windows, straggling behind Kath and Buckley who were walking ahead to where the Kombi was parked.

His indifference, however, vanished when he spotted the cluster of pushbikes on the footpath ahead, and the group of kids who stood nearby. Locals, he realized, and paused long enough to observe their almost similar clothing and country-cut hair; the unnervingly perceptive and knowing expressions their faces seemed to have. *They're no older than me anyway*, he thought to himself, and took a better grip on the bag of groceries. Shoving his free hand into his shorts pocket, moving his mouth up and down as if to chew on an imaginary piece of bubble gum, he walked past the group in an unblinking but not uncaring silence.

'Bloody tourists,' said a chirpy country voice behind him.

17

'Yeah, bloody tourists,' came a chorus of other voices. Their talk seemed to follow him all the way back to the Kombivan, and his mind smarted at the thought of starting school in this town with those kids. Tough, knowledgeable, ridiculing, country kids . . .

What's it going to be like? he wondered, and spent the rest of the weekend thinking about Monday.

Three

Amid the shelter and green confinement of the town was the school.

Suddenly, he was there; not in the safety of the caravan park, but at the school. Standing on a timber verandah, surrounded by the apparent serenity of ageing weatherboard classroom buildings and towering Norfolk pine-trees, he was wishing he could go back to the caravan.

'Breakfast, Trev,' Kath had said that morning.

'I know, Mum.'

'School today ...' He hadn't answered. Grudgingly he had dressed, laboriously he had eaten breakfast. He had taken as long as he could, unconsciously hoping that some miracle would prevent school from commencing.

Public School, 1907. The peeling painted letters had caught Trevor's eye. They stood out, distinct from the rest of the building on which they had been placed, distinct from the cracked weatherboard and fading paint. From the verandah where he stood he could see the entire school – half a dozen identical old buildings placed around a barren asphalt playground, their starkness half masked by the trees and bushes that surrounded each of them. On the asphalt, in a dozen or so orderly lines, were the children of the school in their grey uniforms. Trevor could only see their backs, because they were all facing a rostrum where a teacher was addressing them over a loudhailer. Trevor counted four other teachers, all women, who flanked the assembly lines. The teacher with the loudhailer was the only man, tall and heavily built, with an imposing face and short brown hair. Over the loudhailer his voice sounded efficient and aggressive. His address was punctuated with commands of 'Attention!' and 'Stand at ease!', which the assembled children obeyed with clockwork accuracy.

Public School, 1907. Trevor read it again.

'Some school, huh?' Kath said. She was beside him on the verandah, watching the assembly proceedings with some amusement. She was wearing one of her long, summery dresses and a pair of leather sandals, and her hair was plaited.

Trevor nodded a reply then frowned, looking down at his feet, at the worn verandah boards and the schoolbag beside him. Kath had sewn it, a patchwork shoulderbag made from scraps of calico, velour and denim. Inside it was an exercise book, a half-eaten biro, his lunch. Beside the shoulderbag was his soccer ball. He'd rummaged around in the cupboards under his bunk that morning and found it. He was still debating whether or not he should have brought it along, but as usual he had, because it came with him every time he started at a new school. Bringing it usually meant someone to play with at lunchtime, and maybe even the benefit of a friend or two.

Friends! he thought then, because the morning assembly had finished, and the children were dispersing in lines towards their various classrooms. He was hoping to remain fairly inconspicuous where he was, but the oldest group of children was coming his way. He could see them pointing at him, whispering between themselves and laughing, and the familiar sick feeling began at the pit of his stomach. He hated first days at school and tried angrily to gaze past the advancing group of kids, guessing that this would have to be his new class, since all the others in the playground had

20

been younger grades. And then, with subdued horror, he realized that the man with the loudhailer was following the approaching class. He must be the teacher.

Trevor stood frozen at the verandah railing beside Kath, who seemed to be oblivious to all that he was thinking. The group of kids reached the steps beside them and then filed across the verandah into the adjacent classroom, each of them silently and briefly regarding Kath and Trevor.

The man came up to them then. 'Mrs Huon?' he asked, smiling politely. 'I'm Mr Fuller, headmaster and senior grades teacher . . .' He rambled on to Kath about welcomes and about his school and Trevor listened, disliking the teacher for no apparent reason. When Mr Fuller spoke to him it was to say hullo only, before taking Kath into a small office beside the classroom.

Trevor stood on the verandah alone, wishing it could all be over and done with. Behind him in the classroom was a hum of voices, and every so often his ears heard murmurs of 'new kid . . .'

He thought for a moment of Buckley, who today had started at the bricklaying job. First thing that morning his father had bounced around the caravan like an excited child, dressed in his best work clothes and itching to start at a job he hadn't worked at for a long time.

'Do I look like a good bricklayer?' Buckley had asked, and Trevor momentarily grinned, remembering his and Kath's chorused reply of 'Yuk!'

Kath was next to him again. 'See you later, huh!' she said, climbing down the stairs. 'Have a good day.'

'Yeah, see you,' Trevor managed to reply, watching her go.

The teacher was next to him then, Mr Fuller with his efficient voice. 'You can go inside, Trevor,' he said, indicating the nearby classroom. 'I'll be in in just a moment.'

He walked slowly inside. The hum of conversation abruptly stopped, and fleetingly he saw the groups of faces turned towards his own. He switched his gaze to the floorboards and stood motionless next to the doorway, the soccer ball in one hand, the shoulderbag in the other. Twenty or more of them, boys and girls with sharp country faces, sat frozen behind their desks, watching him in silence.

Trevor was acutely aware of the sea of eyes fixed on him, and vainly tried to focus his mind elsewhere. The teacher still hadn't entered the room, and slowly the hum of conversation resumed.

'Hey, mate,' said a voice, 'how old are you?'

'He's pretty small.'

Ripples of laughter. Trevor remained silent.

'Reckon you're in the wrong class, mate. Kindergarten's the other side of the playground.'

More laughter.

'Jeez, he's quiet. Say something.'

'What's the soccer ball for?'

'You got hair like a girl, mate.'

'Maybe he is . . .'

The talk stopped as the teacher walked into the room, slamming the door shut behind him. 'I don't believe I asked anyone to make a noise,' he said loudly, glaring at the class. 'We have a newcomer, as you may have noticed. Trevor Huon starts here today, and he'll be with us for the next few months.' He turned to Trevor. 'Luckily for you, we have a vacant desk.'

Trevor managed to look up then, self-consciously scanning the neat lines of desks, two rows for boys, two rows for girls. He looked long enough at the class to recognize a few of the faces he'd seen on the Saturday morning, and they looked back at him, smirking.

'Up there at the back, next to Martin Grace.'

Martin Grace obligingly wrinkled his nose in dislike as Trevor started towards the vacant desk. There was another murmur of giggles.

'Some people here seem intent on getting extra homework to do!' the teacher thundered suddenly. There was immediate silence. Mr Fuller indicated to Trevor to stay where he was at the front of the room.

'Before you go anywhere, Trevor Huon,' the teacher said, 'perhaps you'd like to tell us a bit about yourself.'

Oh no, Trevor thought, but shrugged indifferently. In such imposing company, he didn't feel safe refusing. The class was waiting expectantly for him to say something.

'Well,' said Mr Fuller, 'whereabouts in town are you living?'

'The caravan park.'

'The caravan park?' the teacher exclaimed, feigning surprise. 'Have your parents bought the caravan park?'

'No,' Trevor sighed, 'we're just staying there.'

'Do you stay in caravan parks all the time?' the teacher continued.

Trevor moved restlessly. To himself he thought, *stop making fun of me*, but sensed that explanation was the only way to conclude this inquisition and so escape to the vacant desk. 'We live in caravan parks all the time,' he said flatly, looking at the floor. 'We move around all the time depending on where my parents get work.'

The teacher looked back at the class then and said stiffly, 'Thank you, Trevor, you can go and sit down now. Up the back, next to Martin. Good morning, everybody.'

'Good morning sir,' the class chorused back, more intent on Trevor's progress to the vacant desk than on the teacher and the blackboard covered in chalked exercises behind him.

Trevor sat down awkwardly, glancing quickly at Martin Grace, who was still wrinkling his nose.

'Right,' Mr Fuller said, regaining the class's attention once again, 'if I could have everybody facing the front, we'll revise the spelling list.'

Trevor gazed ahead blankly, swept into the confusion of people and work he didn't know. The teacher and the class had a definite routine and they ploughed on relentlessly through spelling lists and exercises, through mathematics that threatened to take all morning to perform and complete. They gave answers in rehearsed unison, they responded briskly to Mr Fuller's rapid-fire questioning and left Trevor to hastily scribble down guessed answers and halfhearted sentences.

'Brad Clark,' said the teacher, 'how many tenths in two?'

'Twenty, sir.'

'Tracy Campbell, how many fifths in five?'

'Um, twenty-five, sir.'

'Michael O'Leary, how many eighths in three?'

'Um . . .'

'Come on,' Mr Fuller shouted, 'you learnt this back in fourth class!'

For a while at least, Trevor found himself excluded from the teacher's attention, and he almost ceased concentrating as the repetitive chanting of mathematical tables filled his ears. His vision was numbed by the dullness of the classroom, at the sight of a few token maps on the bare grey walls, at the boredom of desks in rows. Everything was neat down to a detail, cupboards and shelves were labelled and not a thing seemed out of place. He had been in schools not unlike this before, but somehow this all seemed worse than anything he'd previously experienced.

Beside him, Martin Grace had eased himself as far away from Trevor as was possible, and occasionally muttered audibly, 'You're a sissy, mate.' Away from the teacher's sight, the other boys in the class stole looks at Trevor, copying Martin's nose-wrinkled expressions.

Every so often Trevor glanced sideways at Martin, and Martin always managed a subtle look of disgust as a reply. He was much bigger than Trevor, an arrogant sort of kid with a trail of freckles across his face and close-cropped blond hair. He was obviously not pleased at having a newcomer sitting next to him.

The teacher was beside him. 'You're here to work, Trevor Huon, not to dream. Where are all these maths exercises you're supposed to be doing?'

'Here.' Trevor pointed.

'Here sir!'

'Here sir.'

'Is this the only book you've got?' the teacher asked with some distaste, flicking through the grubby exercise book Trevor had brought along.

'Yes sir.'

'I'll give you a new one. Your writing's awful.'

'My mum says it's good for a left-hander.'

'I want it to improve. Do you hear me?'

'Yes.'

'Yes sir!'

Trevor sighed. 'Yes sir.'

Mercifully, the morning reached an end. Somewhere outside a bell rang and Mr Fuller systematically allowed the kids out, girls first, row by row, and then the boys, led by a kid bouncing a football.

'I'll confiscate that next time, David Briggs.'

'Yes sir.'

Hesitantly, Trevor scooped up his soccer ball from the floor under the desk and followed the class outside into the playground. The boys had gone over to a far corner of the

25

playground, to an open gravelled space between the school buildings where they stood in a broad circle, passing the football around. Clutching the soccer ball in one hand, Trevor walked over to where they stood. Usually, bringing the soccer ball to school worked. But not this time.

One of the kids caught sight of him. 'Hey, this guy plays soccer.'

'Check him out! What a nurd . . .'

'What're you, mate? Only wogs play soccer!'

'Isn't that what he is?'

'Hey, Grace! Your boyfriend here plays soccer.'

'Rack off, Evans! He's not my boyfriend.'

'Well, he sits next to you . . .'

'D' you play league, Trevor whoever you are – Huon?'

'Does he even know how to play?'

Trevor shrugged. 'Not –'

'Aaaah he doesn't know. Soccer freak.'

'The new kid's a soccer freak.'

'C'mon, let's go.' And they ran off to their game of league.

Trevor watched them go, embarrassed and defeated. Some other kids, mostly the girls from his class, had been watching it all happen and were now giggling and talking between themselves. Trevor swore in anger.

Eventually he went and sat down. The sun was shining warmly on to him, and in bemused silence he hugged the useless soccer ball between his feet.

The playground was filled with children, active with their games and their talk. *I hate this place*, he thought. From the seats at the asphalt's edge he watched the boys from his class as they shouted friendly abuse between themselves, kicking their football around and making mad dashes towards imaginary goalposts.

'Don't worry about them,' said a voice beside him. He

looked up and saw a group of girls – Tracy Campbell, plus a few other faces he had heard Mr Fuller put names to that morning. He almost started feeling like an animal in a zoo then, but they started talking to him, conveying towards him a rough, self-conscious sort of sympathy.

'Don't take any notice of them, Trevor.'

'They're always like that. Think they're smart . . .'

'Where d' you come from, Trevor?'

'How many schools have you been to this year?'

'This is the third one,' he managed to answer, with little enthusiasm.

'Jeez, but it's only July!'

'I like your shirt.' Laughter. 'What's it made from? You can see right through it!'

'My mum made it,' he answered.

'Boy, she's clever.'

'Do you like Mr Fuller?'

'Neither do we, don't worry.'

'Your hair's long . . .'

'Mr Fuller likes the boys better, anyway.'

Trevor looked up. 'Why?'

'Because they're all in his football team.'

'He'll probably ask you to join too, Trevor.'

'Fat chance,' Trevor said, looking up at them again. 'He doesn't like me much.'

'That's just Mr Fuller.'

'He's like that.'

'Just don't take any notice.'

He looked down again then, and said nothing. The girls watched him for a moment more, at a loss as to what more to say, and then walked off together, talking between themselves.

He did a lot of thinking that night.

'So how was school?' Kath asked him when he got home.

'All right,' he managed to answer.

'Just all right?'

'Yea, just all right.'

He escaped to the caravan park's amenities block later, and for ages stood under one of the showers. Barbs of hot water rained on his head and back until the cubicle was filled with thick, warm mist.

School puzzled and dismayed him. So the teacher had knocked him about living in the caravan park. That wasn't so bad, because he was fairly used to that. But in the other schools he'd been to, in the orchard and crop towns, there hadn't been just him, but a whole group of pickers' kids. Every year they arrived at the same schools at more or less the same time. The teachers usually considered them nuisances and dunces and sat them in a group, separate from the rest of the class. For all it was annoying to be branded as just another fruitpicker's dumb kid, Trevor decided that it wasn't all that bad, really. At least in those other schools there had been other kids to mix and identify with, to remain fairly anonymous with.

But here, in this town and this school, he was alone and he was different.

Afterwards, he looked critically at himself in the mirror, at the face that seemed too young for eleven years old and the eyes that weren't aggressive enough. His hair was all wrong too, tawny and dangling in wisps on to his shoulders. But that was an individuality he clung to, because he'd worn it that long ever since he could remember.

'And I'm short for my age, too,' he said aloud to the mirror.

Buckley had come home that afternoon with his boots covered in dirt and concrete dust, his face grimy with perspiration; smelling of bricks. He filled the caravan with the mood of a day's work, helping Kath cook dinner as he usually did. They worked as a hectic team, chopping up vegetables and manoeuvring saucepans and frypans around on the caravan's inadequate bench space. Evenings in the caravan were like this, a well-timed confusion. Usually Kath and Buckley sang while they cooked, songs they'd sung hundreds of times and didn't ever seem to get sick of, even if Trevor did. Or maybe there'd be music, old cassettes of Buckley's playing on the portable tape decks on top of the fridge – loud, harsh music that was a swirl of guitars, saxophones and electronic sounds, crazed voices singing obscure lyrics.

More often than not the TV would be on, too, with the news or reruns of American shows interspersed with rural commercials for sheep drench and cattle sales.

'So how was school?' Buckley asked, as the three of them sat around the table eating dinner and half watching the TV. And Trevor offered the same answer he'd given Kath.

He didn't feel like talking much, and afterwards retreated to the privacy of the Kombivan. Once there, he sat on the bunk and gazed in hurt confusion at his makeshift bedroom.

School. Day One finished.

He could hear tentative musical sounds as Kath and Buckley started to play their guitars, and as the darkness of night cloaked the caravan, familiar songs reached Trevor's ears. Briefly reassured, he started to hum along, but there were other things crowding his mind.

Tomorrow would be different. *After today*, he thought grimly, *it would have to be*.

Four

He didn't take the soccer ball to school again. He threw it back into the cupboard under his bunk and there it stayed, along with all the other toys he rarely played with.

'I like your bag, mate. It's really pretty.'

They confronted him in the playground the next day, before school started. He glanced at them long enough to see most of the boys from his class, plus a few extras who were younger. This cohesive, mocking group followed him most of the way to the classroom, delivering various insults as they went. At one point someone made a grab for the patchwork shoulderbag, but Trevor snatched it back and kept walking.

'Hey, he fights back. The new kid's not docile.'

'Where's your soccer ball, Shorty?'

'Yeah, where's your soccer ball?'

'How come your mother isn't here today?'

'My dad reckons only fairies have long hair and play soccer.'

Finally they left him alone, and somehow he made it through the rest of the day. Mr Fuller gave Trevor a set of new, unused exercise books, confiscating the grubby, much-used one brought to school the day before. Dutifully, Trevor wrote down maths exercises and comprehension lessons with the rest of the children in the dim starkness of the classroom. Mutely he sat through the teacher's questioning sessions and afterwards ate alone in the welcome escape of the playground.

The girls came up and talked to him again, offering the same helpful advice.

'Don't take any notice of the boys . . .'

'They just think they're smart.'

'Fuller's a creep, isn't he?'

The advice was interrupted with giggles.

'Hey, Trevor. Angela Simmons loves you.'

'Aw, shut up, I do not!'

'You do so –'

'I don't –'

And they walked off in a giggling embarrassed huddle.

In class, he mulled over what to do. For a few minutes at least he cut himself off from the teacher's deadpan social studies lesson and decided that his initial dislike of Mr Fuller was well founded. Then he cast a furtive eye over the rest of the class, mainly the boys, not fully understanding the reason for his alienation. In some ways it was obvious; he was the newcomer and they were a staunch group of kids who had probably grown up together, bonded by years of common friendship and united against outsiders. But even understanding this Trevor still hotly resented the situation and the treatment he'd received.

It isn't fair, he thought again and again. It was only the second day at this school, yet a lifetime seemed to have dragged by.

He looked sideways at Martin Grace, expecting to see the usual expression of contempt, but for once Martin merely stared back, his freckled face mimicking Trevor's own nonchalant expression.

So far, Martin had saved his talking for the times when he sided with the other kids against Trevor. But now he opened his mouth to speak, only to be silenced as Mr Fuller

31

issued loud instructions from the front of the classroom.

'... using your atlas, fill out the stencil I gave you all yesterday ...'

As the class sank into a hum of activity, Martin took the opportunity to speak, or rather, whisper, loudly: 'What're you staring at, Huon?'

Trevor hesitated, and then whispered back irrelevantly, 'How come you sit by yourself?'

'I don't.'

'You did before I arrived.'

'Well I felt like it, didn't I! You girl.'

'I'm not a girl.'

'How come you wear funny clothes, then?'

'I don't.'

'You do. Weird shirts and things. And that lady's bag you carry around ...'

'It's a shoulderbag. Lots of people have them.'

'Lots of people where? Queer people like you, maybe. My dad says you must be ...'

'Who must be?' Trevor interrupted.

'Your family. Must be strange, my dad says.'

'Your dad doesn't know what he's talking about.'

'Living in a caravan,' Martin retorted triumphantly, 'wearing funny clothes. Moving all over the place.'

'So?' At that moment, Trevor felt a large hand crash down on to his shoulder.

'Where is your social studies book, Trevor Huon?' Mr Fuller boomed.

'Right here. Sir.'

'Well, open it then. Why were you talking?'

'I don't know.'

'Neither do I.' The teacher picked up the open exercise book and promptly dropped it back on to the desk. 'Your writing still hasn't improved.'

The complaint infuriated Trevor. 'I'm left-handed and that's my best writing.'

'It needs improvement. Do something about it.'

The teacher strode away, leaving Trevor staring angrily at his exercise book. *I hate this place*, he thought in exasperation, *because it's July and why aren't Buckley and Kath fruitpicking in . . . where*? he couldn't remember. All he could see was the sanitary classroom, Mr Fuller and, beside him, Martin Grace's mocking grin.

When he came home she was in the caravan, sitting at the table with the sewing machine set up. She smiled at him and said hullo as usual, but he looked at her curiously.

'Have you been sewing all day?'

'Good grief, no,' she said, grimacing. 'Just this afternoon. I spent all morning cleaning up around the place. Gave the Kombi a wash too; did you notice?'

'Yeah, I thought it looked different. How come Dad doesn't take it to work?'

'Well, it's only five or ten minutes' walk to where they're building at the club. He thinks the walk can't do him any harm.' She paused, and then changed the subject. 'And what did you do all day?'

'Nothing.'

'Nothing? You mean to tell me that that teacher of yours with his loud voice is teaching you nothing?'

'Not anything I'd like to learn.'

'Oh,' she replied, and waited for him to elaborate.

'Well, he's too bossy,' Trevor continued. 'Mean, even. I don't like him much.'

'Oh,' she said again. 'What about the other kids?'

'I dunno. The girls think he's a creep. I don't know about the boys.'

'Well,' Kath sighed, 'some people you just have to make

33

allowances for. Teachers included. And we'll be here for at least another two months. Think you'll survive that long?'

'I guess so. I have before.' He stopped to think for a moment. 'It's just,' he said, 'it's just that we've never been here before and I don't know anyone.'

Kath looked at him seriously and sympathetically. 'I know, Trev –'

'Is there anything to eat?' he interrupted. 'I'm kind of starving.'

'Orange juice in the fridge. And you can make yourself a sandwich.'

'Thanks, Mum.'

He went outside afterwards and sat down, his eyes scanning the surrounding caravan park, the town and the late afternoon haze that had settled over the distant slopes. Earnestly he wished he could be elsewhere, not here in this place. But already he could feel himself and his parents locked into a daily routine and he grudgingly accepted the inevitable. They were going to be here for a while.

The boys think they're smart. They're all in Mr Fuller's football team.

Fragments of playground conversation came to mind, and he tried to piece the fragments into a meaningful sort of picture. *All the boys in that class in one team. In what team?*

Finally he stood up and went back into the caravan. Kath had started sewing again, but stopped when he reappeared beside her at the table.

'Mum?'

'Yes?'

'What would you and Dad reckon about me playing football?'

'Don't think we'd mind.'

'I mean, playing in a team.'

34

She thought for a moment. 'Since when were you interested in football? Is it union or league?'

'League.'

'I thought soccer was your only sporting pastime?'

'Yes. No, not really. But if I played in a proper team, what would you and Dad think?'

'We'd think you were nuts. But it's your decision. Why are you asking this all of a sudden?'

'Oh . . . nothing really. I just wondered.'

An impossible scheme had come into his head.

'Where's your soccer ball, Huon?'

'He threw it in the garbage!'

They all laughed then and watched him jokingly, enjoying his normal silence. He looked up at them though, expressionless, but framing sentences to himself, devising responses to what they might say in a moment's time. It had taken several days for him to decide whether to carry out what he had planned. There were rights and wrongs to it, and there was a lot of risk as well.

But I'm sick of them rubbishing me, he thought then, and said: 'I just didn't want to bring the soccer ball to school, that's all.'

'Yeah? Isn't soccer the only game you know how to play?'

'No.'

'You couldn't kick a football as far as you could blow your nose.'

'Yes I could.'

'Bet you can't.'

'I can.'

'When have you ever played football?'

The story he'd planned came out smoothly. 'Where I used to live,' Trevor said.

35

'Where was that?'

'In the city.'

'Bet it wasn't proper footy.'

'I played on a school team.'

The group watched him, unbelieving. The questions continued.

'Yeah? What position did y' play?'

'Um, back.'

'Then how come you've only got a soccer ball?'

'I got sick of playing football.'

The kids retained their element of suspicion.

'I reckon you're telling us a lot of crap, Huon.'

'Yeah, you couldn't play football anyway. You're too little.'

The last comment sent the group into fits of giggles. Trevor watched them, debating whether to forget the whole thing or whether to keep going. He flushed angrily. 'Well if you don't believe me, why don't you let me play?'

The kids looked at each other.

'You're too little,' one of them said. 'The ball's bigger than you are.'

'No, let's see him play.'

'Yeah, come on.'

'See if he's lying or not –'

'But fairies can't play footy.'

'Shut up, Jason. Let him play.'

Confident and grinning, they split into two teams of seven and found themselves appropriate positions on the dusty paddock of the lower playground. In his solitary position as left winger, Trevor almost smiled to himself, but it was a mixture of confidence and doubt that rested heavily on him at that instant. He'd lied his way into a game with the kids successfully, but it was now a tough matter of saving face.

After all, league football was a largely unknown quantity. Then his smile dimmed into apprehension as the ball was kicked off and play began.

Because the teams were small the game could have been a highly informal one, but it was played in a professional and cunning manner. Trevor found that the ball was passed to him a great deal. He made a stubborn effort to look experienced, but played nervously.

'You don't know how to play,' Martin Grace said to him.

'I'm just out of practice, aren't I?' Trevor hissed back, and kept running.

At first he really had little idea of the mechanics of the game, but with a bit of careful observation was able to bluff his way through. But the going was hard. Towards the end, the game seemed to comprise not two, but three teams – the third team being Trevor, with the other two teams united against him. Whenever he got the ball, they came at him from all directions, blocking his path, trying to trip him up, attempting to wrestle the ball from his grasp.

Finally, the end-of-lunchtime bell rang in the playground. Slowly and mercifully, the game came to a standstill.

'Now d' you believe me?'

The other kids looked at him. 'You're not a very good player,' someone sneered, but no one else took up the argument at that moment.

'Are you playing again tomorrow?' Trevor asked as they walked back to the classroom.

They exchanged unwilling looks.

'What if we are, Huon?'

'Yeah, what if we are?'

He tried to sound assertive. 'Well, can I play then?'

Again, they all seemed to exchange expressions. It was

like a secret code between them, and it took until they were stepping into the classroom for a reply to be made. Or rather, a challenge.

'On one condition, Huon.'

'What's that?' Trevor asked cautiously.

'That you join the team we're in.'

'What team?' Trevor started to ask, but the other kids had broken into derisive laughter.

'Get out of it, Brad! He couldn't make the team.'

'No way!'

'He's too little –'

'He can hardly play –'

Trevor raised his voice defiantly: 'All right. I'll join.'

They regarded him with cynical interest.

'You're gutless, Huon. You won't join.'

'Yes I will.'

'Bet you won't,' said Martin Grace.

'Bet I will.'

'Any money you won't.'

'Any money I will.'

By now, the others had caught the new drift of the conversation, and clustered around Trevor, offering challenges again, but explanations as well.

'Our team's the best in the district . . .'

'Rack off! Best in the state . . .'

'You're not good enough, Huon. Admit it.'

'We're a hard team to beat.'

'Won the comp two years running!'

'Mr Fuller's the coach. He's pretty tough.'

'Too tough for you, Huon.'

Through all this Trevor sat at his desk, patiently and silently listening to what they were saying. The apparent success of his lying washed over him, but it wasn't a happy feeling; at least, not yet. The kids were binding him with conditions, blocking the way out of his isolation and maybe even suspecting his real lack of experience.

What happens next? he thought. There were doubts that persisted, and he felt totally out of his depth.

At that moment Mr Fuller strode into the room, and the kids turned their attention from Trevor to the teacher.

'Hey, sir, Trevor Huon wants to join the football team.'

Mr Fuller looked at Trevor with brief interest. 'You've played before?'

'Yes,' Trevor gulped.

'Well, our next training session's tomorrow afternoon, after school. I'm sure Martin Grace will fill you in on the details.'

'Sure, sir,' Martin answered, grinning sarcastically.

Trevor felt trapped.

Five

They were waiting for him the next day after school, grouped in a derisive huddle on the stretch of playing field behind the weatherboard classrooms.

His arrival was cheered mockingly.

'Hey, he's here . . .'

'Where's your soccer ball, Huon?'

'You gonna train with us or just watch?'

'Watch him drop from exhaustion after five minutes!'

By now, he knew most of them by name. Martin Grace aside, there were Bradley, Michael, David, Rob, Peter, Scott, Jason, another Peter, Andrew, Damian and a few others he couldn't quite remember. The one who seemed to do much of the talking was Bradley Clark, who prided himself as the team's star player, and occasionally liked reminding the other kids of this fact. He had scored the most points that season, had kicked the most impressive field goals and made marathon dashes towards try lines.

And then there was Mr Fuller.

Local powers-that-be had awarded him the authority of manager and coach of the town's starring junior football team, and it was a dual responsibility he did not appear to take lightly. When he arrived on the playing field to take command of the hour's training session, he struck Trevor as looking strangely incongruous. The man who dressed so soberly for the classroom now wore a T-shirt, shorts and running shoes. His personality, however, remained unchanged.

He quickly sighted Trevor amongst the other familiar team faces.

'So you decided to come along,' Fuller said grimly, and then addressed the kids collectively. 'It appears that we have a new team member. Trevor Huon has decided to grace us with his diminutive presence. How old are you, Huon?'

'Eleven.'

'I don't believe you.' The other kids caught the dig at Trevor's lack of height, and laughed accordingly.

'Almost twelve,' Trevor added for safety. He was coming to dislike Fuller more and more; the face, the bulging stomach, the sweaty shirt, the impatient critical eyes and the voice most of all.

Fuller was talking again. 'I'm going to lay this on the line, young Huon – you're a risk, I hope you realize that. We're most of the way through the season competition, and haven't lost a game yet. Taking on a new player at this stage isn't on, and we've already got two reserves. So we don't really need you. But believe me, you'll have to train as hard as the rest of us. This team's won the district competition two years running and we're working hard to make this our third. Get that, Huon?'

'Yes.'

'Yes sir!'

'Yes sir.'

'I'm not having a newcomer mucking things up. Previous experience you've had of course. What team was that?'

Trevor's mind raced for an answer, and he eventually provided a suitable reply. 'Penrith Under Elevens,' he said.

'Position?' Fuller snapped.

'Five eighth,' Trevor answered mechanically. This much he'd managed to find out from Buckley.

'And what does a five eighth do, Huon?'

'Um, he takes the first pass off the half back . . .'

Fuller sighed audibly and interrupted, 'When he gets the ball from the half, he has to decide whether to initiate some back movement through the centres, or turn and play back inside to the forwards. He must *always* back up the running forwards who make a break. Get it?'

'Yes. Sir,' mumbled Trevor, frantically trying to assimilate all the technical information.

'We could use a tactical kicker,' Fuller continued, 'but time will tell, won't it Huon?' He paused and looked hard at Trevor, then turned his attention to the rest of the team. 'And this week, I want some sweat! Last week was such a bludge that the Colts got within three points. Disgusting! This week, we're going to have some real training. Twice around the oval for starters. Get moving!'

Running forwards, running backwards, flexing arms, legs, feet, doing push-ups and sit-ups in an icy sweat, exercise Trevor wasn't quite used to. Running again, more push-ups, and lots of shouting to accompany the team's efforts.

'Get those feet up. Legs straight! Come on, Under Twelve Blobs! Do we want to be beaten next week?'

It was a mechanical sort of question, which received a mechanical sort of reply. 'NO!' the team chorused, in between Touching Toes Without Bending Knees.

They played touch football then, running headlong in a frenetic parody of the real thing. Trevor found himself in the midst of the shouting mob, all of them passing the leather football amongst themselves. In an instant, he found the ball in his own hands and frantically searched around for someone to pass it on to.

'Get that ball out, Huon!' came the shout from the edge of the field.

Gingerly, Trevor passed it out.

Fuller was shouting again. 'Stop! Everybody stop!'

They came to a heaving standstill.

'Huon,' Fuller said in a loud, exasperated voice, 'this is a football team I am in charge of here. Not a bunch of fairies. You are not handing out boiled lollies to the team, you are passing a football. Now do it quickly, do it well, or go home.'

They started running again. Somewhere beside him, he could hear the thump of the ball being passed out once more.

'Huon!' This time it was Martin who called. He had the ball, and promptly slung it towards Trevor's outstretched hands. This time Trevor passed the ball swiftly on to the kid who was running next to him. There was no reaction from Fuller.

The practice continued, with a few variations. Fuller threw an extra ball on to the field and the team dispersed in two groups towards two sets of goalposts to practise set moves.

Trevor's confidence ebbed as Fuller strode up to watch. When it was his turn he kicked badly, and the football spun off at a tangent, missing the goalposts by a mile.

'Huon,' Fuller said edgily, 'did I hear you say you'd played football before?'

'Yes,' Trevor answered, gritting his teeth and almost feeling like giving in. 'I'm just out of practice.'

'Well get into practice quick smart. I want a big improvement from you before you associate further with my team. You can come to training tomorrow and all next week, and start as third reserve at next week's game. But improve, boy.'

Fuller turned to go, but then remembered something else. Sternly, he pointed at what Trevor was wearing. 'That isn't proper training gear. You're *not* fronting up for sessions dressed like you're going to the beach. Or to school, in your case. I want to see a proper T-shirt and sandshoes or gymboots, not bare feet. And do something with your hair. Tie it back or better still, get it cut. How do you expect to see what you're doing with it all over your face?'

And so it went on. The criticism was inevitable and wearing. The training session dragged on.

When at last it was over Martin Grace said, 'Boy, Fuller doesn't like you much.'

There was an odd sympathy to his voice, which intrigued Trevor. In fact, he found Martin generally intriguing, because there were times when he seemed to act and think differently from the other kids. Trevor couldn't pinpoint exactly why or how this was so.

He made a face. 'I guess Fuller just doesn't want me around.'

'He's always like that.' Martin added with the voice of a hardened veteran, 'You should know that by now. We're the only team in the whole town that has to train three times a week. Other teams only train twice. And we always train by ourselves here at school, not down on the town oval like everyone else.'

'Why? Because you win so much?'

'Yeah, I guess so.'

Me and my stories, Trevor thought angrily to himself, knowing he was caught well and truly now. He was a mixture of emotions. He almost wanted to forget the whole thing, but his pride wasn't going to let his stories of football expertise down.

Slowly, a routine established itself.

44

Each day, five days a week, Buckley went to work on the building site at the club. He came home in the evenings with stories of the men he worked with, cynical local contractors who considered Buckley odd because he didn't go with them after work for drinks at the Lindsay Hotel.

Kath's 'break' from a paid job seemed to be no holiday. During the day she busied herself making clothes or spinning wool for future knitting projects. She went for long, rambling walks around the township and its fringes, and as the days passed her insights into the workings of this particular country town collaborated with Buckley's to form a telling picture of the people who lived there.

Inconveniently distant from larger places, the town had assumed a stifling lifestyle of its own. For entertainment you went to the Lindsay Hotel, or better still, to the club, a place where farmers, timber mill workers and the general adult population congregated to drink, talk and gamble away money on the poker machines.

The club, ever mindful of the younger population, ran its own little network of sporting teams for the local kids, which was where Fuller's Under Twelves fitted in. Sport wasn't a full-time affair, however, and there was often little to do after school hours, unless you paid money to play the pinball machines at the local milkbar, or saw the occasional movie at the small, museum-like cinema. Groups of schoolkids wandered aimlessly about at the weekends, and carloads of teenagers stationed themselves outside the life-support of the milkbar.

Buckley and Kath maintained a quiet distance from these social offerings. Trevor, of course, did not.

'What d' you do in a caravan all day?' Martin wanted to know. 'I'd be bored silly.'

Somehow, Trevor had always found something to do. He explored, like his mother. He played solo card games

45

and sometimes Monopoly with his parents till all hours of the night. He helped Buckley when the Kombivan needed servicing and repairs. And he daydreamed a lot. Impossible thoughts and imaginary stories found their way into his mind all the time, and he projected himself wholeheartedly into such fantasies, which more often than not were about anything but living in a caravan and being the son of two slightly crazy seasonal workers.

But now, the life of the town had engulfed most of these interests, such as they were. A new routine had settled itself upon him, and three afternoons a week he trained with Fuller and the team, reluctantly determined to put some truth into his stories of football glory.

It was a process that exhausted him.

Seeing so much of Fuller during the week was tense stuff and he had been unprepared for the sudden, exhausting exercise of training. Buckley and Kath remained unconvinced of any benefits to be reaped by Trevor from being a part of that gruelling little institution called the Club Under Twelves. The judgement was based on their own sharp intuition, but it was a decision they allowed Trevor to make for himself.

Kath took him shopping one day to buy the necessary football gear.

'Hope you don't mind not getting new stuff,' she said, as they sorted through piles of secondhand clothing in the local church-run opportunity shop.

He shook his head. It didn't matter in the slightest.

Eventually they found several pairs of shorts and woollen footy socks, the correct team jersey and miraculously, a pair of proper football boots that actually fitted him.

He changed into the ensemble and looked at himself, sports-clad, in the shop mirror. He stared for several moments at the reflection in the glass, not out of vanity, but purely out of interest and curiosity.

'What are you thinking about?' Kath asked with a faint smile, well knowing his daydreaming habits.

'Nothing,' he answered slowly, wishing silently that he was somewhere else, away from this town and its people.

Six

His own family, of course, was different.

It was something he had started to put a lot of thought into, because the differences had suddenly become clearer against the background of the town and the school.

There were the obvious things such as the caravan, the Kombi and the moving around, but that wasn't all. For a long time he had been able to see that Kath and Buckley were intrinsically different from a lot of other parents that he saw, and that was no means a conclusion based on appearance alone. He considered his gaggle of city cousins who were mostly younger than he, and whom he rarely saw. Their parents seemed to spend a lot of time bossing them around and telling them not to be silly. Their parents seemed to have lots of Rules For Behaving and always went slightly mental if these rules were not strictly adhered to. There were other things as well that Trevor couldn't readily identify, but that he knew set his own parents apart from others.

Buckley and Kath, he finally decided, were more like people and less like parents.

But now, there were vague dissatisfactions looming about him. The town had put him out of his depth, school was demanding and intimidating.

The past had a sudden, urgent attraction for him, and he had to find out more.

'There were houses everywhere, no bush at all, one or two small parks . . .' Buckley told him.

Trevor tried to imagine his father as a child, this person now stranded in a country town.

'... by the time I'd finished school, I was sick of the whole polluted, populated mess. So I bought the Kombi, packed food, clothes, guitar, surfboard and a toothbrush. And just drove away.'

'Where to?' Trevor asked.

'Up north.'

'To where we lived?'

'Much further still. Kath, and the house, came later on.'

Delving into the past was piecing together a jigsaw.

'I'm going to travel someday,' Trevor resolved then, 'and go places we haven't been to yet.'

There were albums of photographs, pictures of landscapes crossed within Trevor's lifetime. The places were different, the seasons coloured the Polaroid prints in a cycle of pages. Always, there seemed to be the backdrop of camping grounds and fruitpickers' huts. There was the array of possessions carried in the caravan and the Kombi, such as the surfboard, which Trevor could barely remember his father having used. To this one possession, he attached the most important of his vague recollections, because its links were closely entwined with a house that had once been home.

'Kath taught for a while, of course,' Buckley said. 'You've seen those photos, I guess.'

Trevor nodded. 'What were you doing then?'

'Me? Fixing up cars and motorbikes. Bumming around. Surfing. Renovating your grandmother's house ...'

'Oh.'

Sometimes when in thought, Trevor would look up at Buckley pensively and quizzically, and find his father already gazing at him the same way – as though they had both stopped simultaneously to evaluate a common thought or feeling.

'Dad?'

'Yes?'

'You remember when I was, um, seven, and you told me I could have the Kombi when I'm old enough to drive?'

'Yes. Go on.'

'Well, are you still going to?'

'Well, yes. You've got a while to wait, though.'

'Are you selling it to me or giving it to me?'

'That depends. No, I've just decided to sell it to you.'

'Aw, Dad!'

'Ten thousand dollars. Take it or leave it.'

'But it's twenty years old.'

'So?'

'It might not be working by then.'

'It's been round the clock twice.'

'So? Besides, ten thousand is a ripoff, I reckon.'

'But it's almost an antique,' Buckley said in mock protest.

Pause.

'Hey, c'mon Dad. You said you'd give it to me. No, not said, *promised*. I remember . . .'

Buckley laughed. 'Okay, okay, I'm pulling your leg, dummy. I did promise; what a dumb thing to promise in the first place. The Kombi's yours in about six or seven years' time.' Then he added, 'You've got a memory like a bloody elephant's.'

'Dad?'

'What now?'

'Can you teach me to play guitar some time?'

Buckley shrugged. 'What happened last time, though?'

'I gave up. Because my fingers hurt from pressing the strings down.'

'Mm. When are you going to find time to practise? Guitar is something you have to work at.'

'I know. Can you teach me?'

'Yes,' Buckley said with an obliging sigh, 'I'll teach you. Again. When would you like to start?'

'Tonight?'

'All right. Tonight. But will you have time to practise?'

'Yes.'

'In between football, school and homework from the beloved Mr Fuller?'

'Er, yuk. I mean, yes.'

'And while we're at it, how was school today?'

School.

School was being trapped in the limbo of the classroom all day long while Mr Fuller alternately 'taught' and shouted commands. It was avoiding the teacher's gaze and attention. It was joining in the games of playground football, the benefit of which the other kids now reluctantly allowed him. It was being desk neighbours with Martin Grace.

'Jeez, you wear queer clothes, Huon.'

'I do not.'

'You do. How come you don't dress like everybody else?'

'Because –'

'Because why? I reckon you're a pansy. Mum's boy.'

'Am not.'

'Are so. Wish I didn't have to sit next to you.'

'How come you were sitting by yourself in the first place, then?' Trevor asked with impulsive cruelty. 'Doesn't anyone else like you?'

'You think you're smart, don't you Huon?'

'No.'

'Well I'll tell you why. It's because I'm repeating sixth

51

class. I've had Fuller for a teacher now for three years running. Bet you couldn't handle that.'

'How come you're here for an extra year then?'

'Because I wasn't old enough.'

'You look old enough,' Trevor said suddenly. 'You're taller than the other kids.'

Martin's aggression remained unabated. 'Well I'm not older, am I? And when Fuller let us choose where we wanted to sit at the start of the year, all the kids I was real good friends with had already gone to high school. And now I have to sit next to you. Bloody pansy.'

And so it went on, day after school-bound day. Martin taunting and harping about the same things and Trevor usually giving up and keeping quiet, because Martin was mercilessly persistent. If it wasn't in front of the other kids in the playground, it was in the classroom, in a furtive whisper that usually seemed to escape the teacher's attention. Inside, Trevor fumed at the insults.

What's so good about being like Martin anyway, and living in a slack country town like this? he thought to himself. Buckley, Kath, the Kombi, the caravan – he had a pride in them and stubbornly refused to change wholeheartedly to satisfy the likes of Martin Grace.

'School?' Trevor replied to Buckley. 'It's okay, I guess.'

He realized then that he had his own sort of secretiveness and that there was much of his life that his parents didn't know about. The individuality and small measure of privacy was reciprocal.

And then he thought about Mr Fuller.

That morning the teacher had been occupying his favourite spot beside the blackboard. His eyes scanned the classroom and finding no cause for reprimand he began to address them.

It was the preamble to a lesson.

'. . . and I've decided that our next class assignment will take the form of something creative. I know you've got imagination, at least most of you have. We manage to produce some good artwork one way and another. And lately, the written expression has improved. Michael O'Leary, stop talking! The compositions and poems you've written in your books have been . . . good. Therefore, your next class project takes the form of a written story. Not just a composition, but a story. It can have chapters if you wish.'

'How long does it have to be, sir?' someone asked.

'At least six pages.'

Such lengths were unheard of and the kids made a few appropriately disgruntled noises.

'Remember, it's a story. Your own ideas and not something from T V.'

'When do we start, sir?'

'Today. To be handed in Monday fortnight. You'll have two and a half weeks to work on it, which I tend to think is too long, but two and a half weeks it is. I'll give you some time to think about it now. Written expression books out, everyone.'

'Please sir, can we talk about it?'

'Yes,' Mr Fuller answered generously, 'you may have ten minutes to discuss it amongst yourselves. Quietly.'

'Sir, can it be something about magic?'

'That's imaginary, isn't it Evans?'

'Yes, sir.'

'Well then. Do some thinking, son.'

The classroom was lost to sudden informality. As the conversation buzzed around him, Trevor pondered the form his own expressive contribution might take.

'Hey,' Martin said suddenly, 'd' you like science fiction?'

'Yeah,' Trevor said, 'I've read a couple of my dad's paperbacks.'

'Well, I might write a science fiction story. What are you doing for a story?'

'Dunno.'

Martin looked at him for a moment. 'I know what you can write about, Trevor.'

'What?'

'A fairy story!' said Martin and immediately doubled up giggling at his own profound sense of humour.

Trevor grimaced, knowing that he should have expected such a comment from Martin, who was still engulfed in giggles. Then abruptly, it dawned on Trevor as remotely funny too, and he grinned.

Much later, he lay awake on his bunk in the Kombi. The fingers on his left hand smarted from the renewed efforts at learning the guitar. Inside the caravan his parents were playing familiar songs and he tried not to think about school, but to concentrate on these songs, that he'd known ever since he could remember.

But somehow, images of Mr Fuller, Martin Grace and the kids at school kept coming to mind instead.

Seven

'I just reckon you've been sucked in.'

'Why?'

Martin's voice was condescending, knowing. 'I just reckon you have.'

Trevor was defensive. 'But how d' you know?'

'Look, Huon, I know. You heard what Fuller said. You'll be sitting on that sideline till doomsday. He doesn't trust you, he doesn't even like you.'

'Well I'm not giving up.'

'I think you're stupid.'

'Am not.'

'Nuts!'

'You think I'm really dumb, don't you?'

'No. Yes, a bit. If I was you, I'd call it quits.'

'Well I'm not going to.'

'You've really been sucked in, haven't you?'

The playing field was transformed. The goalposts had been wrapped in team colour streamers and everywhere there were people. It was Saturday afternoon, a day in the very height of the football season. From first thing in the morning till well into the afternoon, the parents came to watch the progression of club football matches played on the two or three adjoining grounds behind the club premises.

Each week, opposing teams of kids would arrive by bus or in cars to play the local teams. The spectrum of ages was wide. There were even teams of little four and five year olds, who struggled across the length and breadth of the field and occasionally stopped altogether, forgetting that it was a serious game they were supposed to be playing. Forgetting, that is, until eager parents yelled at them from the sidelines to get moving, or else.

No other sporting events throughout the year attracted as much attention as the kids' football matches. The girls' matches of basketball, hockey and softball paled by comparison, because the sporting atmosphere of the town was arrogantly and almost exclusively, male.

The noisiest members of the football-watching population were the parents, who took it in unconscious shifts throughout the day to provide a deafening commentary on what their respective sons could be doing to improve the score of each game. Parents arrived with younger children, grandparents and other relative appendages to sit a game out on collapsible chairs positioned along the sidelines. To make things even more comfortable they brought picnic lunches and liquid refreshments in eskys to last the spectating distance, while their sons laboured athletically after a football and an appropriately resounding victory.

This mammoth gathering happened each Saturday, and its fervour was very near religious.

Curiously, Trevor regarded the audience of parents. He wondered what it'd be like to have some of these as mother and father instead of Kath and Buckley, who looked slightly out of place at such an event. They sat cross-legged on the ground and looked around with interest and some amusement, occasionally making wisecrack remarks to each other about any unsuspecting person who happened to attract their attention. Briefly, Trevor felt glad that he had the parents that he did. The others he saw all seemed to have loud voices and an iron grip over their respective

56

broods of children. With subtle glee, he gradually matched a lot of the parents up with the kids from Fuller's team, wondering what it would be like to be Martin Grace or Bradley Clark.

For a while he sat with Kath and Buckley, checking at intervals that the football boots were laced and tied up properly, and that the woollen socks hadn't slithered down to his ankles.

'What do reserves do?' Kath asked.

'They sit on the sidelines and wait,' Trevor answered flatly.

'Is that all?'

'Yeah.'

'And we're supposed to scream, yell, cheer and carry on like all these other parents?'

'If you want to. But you can go home though, if you like,' Trevor continued with a note of resignation. 'It's not as if I'll be doing anything exciting.'

Eventually he stood up and walked over to where the team had begun to assemble nearby. With rehearsed professionalism, they discussed tactics and evaluated the team they were to play against. This opposition was assembled on the other side of the field and appeared to be going through the same process.

'They look easy to beat,' said Michael O'Leary.

'Yeah, we'll walk all over them.'

'That big guy with the black hair looks mean.'

'Which one?'

'Um, number eight.'

'Reckon. Might be hard to tackle.'

'Aw rubbish. Just hammer him in the guts and he'll go down like a ton of bricks.'

Trevor maintained an uncomfortable distance from the team, but their scanning gazes soon found him.

'Hey, the star reserve's here!'

'What's that you've got around your head, Huon?'

'You look like a red indian!'

'It's a headband,' Trevor said, trying to sound coolly indifferent.

'Aw yeah. To keep the hair outa your face when you're scoring us tries.'

'Maybe you should've plaited your hair instead,' said Bradley Clark.

'Maybe you should plait your tongue, Clark,' said Martin Grace, and everybody laughed.

Fuller arrived, cast a swift inspecting look over the team, and began checking off names.

'Anderson?'

'Here.'

'Barnes?'

'Here.'

'Briggs?'

'Here.'

'Clark?'

'Here.'

'Davies . . .?'

Surrounding parents offered a backdrop of advice.

'Don't you forget our agreement, Michael . . .'

'One dollar for every try, Bradley!'

'Run them into the ground, Damian. Tackle them hard.'

'Just show them who the winners are. No TV for a week if you don't.'

'And fifty cents for each field goal, Brad.'

Within earshot, Kath and Buckley exchanged horrified, sympathetically amused looks.

Fuller, meanwhile, launched into what he considered the most important of preambles to any football game: the pep talk to the team. He loaded his speech with emotion and aggression. He was masterly at talking the kids into a winning state of mind, and played on the shame associated with defeat.

'... just remember to get that ball passed out. You second rowers were just too slow last week. It's up to us to have that ball in our possession as often as possible. Remember, the eyes of the town are here watching you. You're a winning team out there, so let's see some action today.' His voice became a calculating half-shout. 'See those guys over there?' he asked, indicating the opposing team who on their side of the field appeared to be receiving much the same sort of rave from their coach. 'See that team over there? They just haven't a chance, as far as I'm concerned. Are we going to win or lose?'

'WIN!' came the team's chorused reply.

'And we're going to remain undefeated. Right?'

'RIGHT!'

'You're going to tackle those guys hard and you're going to move fast and score points. And we'll go on to win the football competition for the third year in a row. Who's the best team in the district?'

'CLUB UNDER TWELVES!' the team shouted back, and sprinted across the sidelines on to the field.

With a substantially smaller allocation of the glory for the three reserves – Jason Evans, Andrew Willis, and Trevor – retired to sit on the reserve bench, which was behind the halfway line and beside the bucket of half-time oranges.

In silence they watched as the two uniformed teams positioned themselves across the field. The spectators assumed an expectant silence, then came to life when the ball was kicked into play.

'Come on, Club!'

'Rub their noses in it!'

'Get him, Scott!'

Nearby, Kath and Buckley remained seated on the grass, surrounded by the raucous enthusiasm of the other parents. They watched the proceedings with the detached interest of people who didn't quite know what was going on. Buckley was occupying himself pulling grotesque faces for the amusement of a couple of younger children who belonged to one set of particularly vocal parents.

'Hey,' said Jason Evans, 'I heard your dad's got a weird first name. What is it?'

'Buckley, you mean?' Trevor asked.

'Yeah.'

'It's his middle name, but he uses it as his first.'

'How come? That's bloody weird, if you ask me.'

Trevor shrugged. 'His first name's really Craig. He just figured Buckley sounded a bit more suave.'

'Sounds weird to me. Hey, look. Brad's going for the try line! Come on, Brad!'

Trevor watched with slight interest. He was being careful to watch the game as it progressed in the hope of picking up a few playing hints to apply himself in the future, but his thoughts wandered. What caught his attention the most was the amusing sight of Fuller striding up and down the sideline, shouting advice to the team, and occasionally, abuse.

'You're leading!' he yelled. 'No excuse for dropping that ball, Anderson!'

'Fuller really goes mental, doesn't he?' Trevor said.

'Yeah, does he what,' Jason answered, and grinned.

It was consistently intriguing to compare this Fuller with the person who occupied the stark classroom at school. Suddenly Trevor remembered the writing assignment, and thought over ideas that could suitably fill enough exercise book pages. With the audience noise behind him and the

60

action of the football game in front, he temporarily re-
moved himself to an imaginary level, until ideas began to
fall into place. He resolved to write them down when he got
home.

Kath and Buckley meanwhile, had been reluctantly
drawn into conversation with somebody's mother.

'And who's your son?' the woman asked. 'I don't think
I've seen you here before.'

'Oh, we're new here,' Kath answered politely. 'Our son's
Trevor. He's just joined the team.'

'Oh, yes,' the woman nodded. 'I believe he's had some
experience with other teams.'

Kath and Buckley looked perplexed. 'No, he's never
played in an organized team before,' Buckley answered.
'This is his first time.'

'Oh,' said the woman, with controlled surprise.

Trevor was out of earshot.

At half-time, the team left the field to regain their energy
over mouthfuls of orange. They had gained a comfortable
lead over the opposition, and Fuller and a few of the
parents mingled with the kids and renewed their varying
advice in loud tones.

Martin and Trevor stood a short distance from the
group.

'The kids still think you're a sissy,' said Martin.

'Stuff them,' Trevor said, shrugging, because the comments were starting to neither worry nor upset him.

'They think you're a bit of a nut,' Martin added.

Trevor took a large bite out of his orange, and chewing
it slowly stared thoughtfully at Martin. 'Do you think I'm
stupid?'

It was Martin's turn to be thoughtful. 'No, I guess not
really,' he said finally, 'but that's only because I think I
know something else.'

'Like what?' Trevor asked.

'Like ...' Martin turned around to see if anyone was listening, 'you've never played football before, have you? In a proper team, like you said?'

Halfway through another mouthful, Trevor stopped chewing and started feeling a bit sick.

'Have you?' Martin asked again.

'No,' Trevor finally answered.

'I didn't think so,' Martin said.

'But how did you know?'

Martin wrinkled his nose. 'I just guessed. I'm not stupid, y' know.'

'Will you tell anyone?'

Martin thought for a moment. 'No,' he answered.

Eight

'Winter's well and truly with us,' Kath said, giving Trevor his thickest jumper to wear to school.

But the day was to become more than cold, because as the Friday afternoon wore on the wind began to lash at the town and the sky filled with heavy black cloud.

It was an ominous prelude to the last training session before the weekend match. With the chill sweeping across the expanse of the oval, the team huddled together on the sideline, and everyone seemed to be wearing tracksuits over the usual shorts and jerseys in an effort to keep warm.

Martin was making flippant references to the coming match.

'Should be an easy game,' he said, holding his folded arms to his chest for warmth. 'We put heaps on that team last time.' But nobody pursued the conversation. They weren't over keen to do anything much, except perhaps to go home.

'Fuller's late.'

'Maybe we're early.'

'Huh!'

'Be nice if training gets called off today.'

But at that moment, a car pulled up beside the boundary fence and a familiar figure stepped out. As if on cue, the black clouds gave way and rain started to fall.

There was a chorus of groans.

'What's wrong with you lot?' Fuller demanded when he

reached them. He had an overcoat on and a large black umbrella perched above his head. 'Get those pyjama things off.' He jabbed an impatient finger at the tracksuits. More groans.

The rain drummed louder and louder on to the open umbrella and, with it, Fuller's voice seemed to get louder. 'Right, get moving!' he commanded.

'Where, Mr Fuller?'

'Around the oval, of course. Jogging!'

'How many times?'

'Until I tell you to stop!'

The rain continued to fall, and bare heads and jerseys were getting wetter by the second. The team set off in a reluctant jog.

'Lift those feet!' came the voice behind them. 'A bit more speed.'

Fuller seemed more impatient than usual. In fact, he'd been like this all day, giving everyone a hard time at school. The weather didn't seem to be worrying him too much, equipped as he was with overcoat and umbrella. But his impatience had an edge of real anger about it today, and even now his voice was rarely dropping below a half-shout. Something seemed set to happen.

The team, if they noticed this at all, weren't going to say much. The drizzle of rain had reduced them to subdued irritation.

'You cold, Scotty?'

'Freezing. My legs are gonna drop off any minute.'

'Shut up, McKay! Maybe Fuller'll let us off early.'

'Huh. Maybe.'

Any other day it would have been a mere warmup, but the jog today was cold and exhausting. Each lap of the oval seemed more like three, and each time they passed by Fuller with his umbrella they were commanded on.

'Another lap, Under Twelves. Keep those feet going!'

So they ran on, a wet, straggling bunch of fed-up kids.
Martin tried relieving the boredom.

'Come on, Huon. You're weak!'

Trevor was too breathless to respond. He shot Martin a
reproachful glance, and concentrated on keeping up with
everyone else.

'Your legs are too short, Huon.'

'So's the rest of him,' someone else added. At this, the
team almost found an excuse for laughter, but instead were
silenced by Fuller's glare as they passed him yet again. The
rain still drizzled and the ground turned to mud beneath
their feet. They even lost count of the number of laps they'd
managed to run around the oval. Each time around became
slower and slower, until Fuller cut the exercise short.

'What's the matter, then?' he called to the team as they
assembled wearily nearby. 'A few of us can't take it, eh?
What happens when we're playing the big game and it
starts raining? You bunch of flowers wouldn't last till half-
time.'

The team regarded him silently. Today they were not in
the mood for pep talks; that could wait until the Saturday
match.

Meanwhile, parents had begun to arrive, thinking that
the rain would bring training to an early finish. They
assembled with raincoats and umbrellas at the boundary
fence, and amid the huddle of cars and mums, Trevor could
see the Kombi.

But Fuller was not finished. 'Right!' he said crisply, 'I
want to see two even lines. Facing me.'

Uncertain of what was to happen, the team lined up.

'Mr Fuller,' someone said, 'can we put our tracksuits
back on?'

'No!' he shouted back. 'Not until I've finished.' His eyes

swept across the silent group and the kids in turn watched him expectantly, waiting for whatever was to be said. For a minute or more this silence was maintained.

The rain came to a stop and Fuller slowly and methodically closed his black umbrella and laid it carefully on the ground. He renewed his icy stare then, looking without expression at the bedraggled team with their rain-soaked hair and faces, listening to the undercurrent of post-jogging puffing and breathing.

At last he spoke. 'A fine lot you are –' although it was irrelevant to what was to follow. He shot them another icy look. 'I thought you might all like to know something,' he added. 'It has recently come to my attention that we have a troublemaker of sorts on our hands.'

He paused for a moment. The team returned his stare.

'To put it more simply, one of you is a liar.'

A few pairs of eyes instantly seemed to search out Trevor, who was standing in the back row beside Martin Grace.

Fuller continued. 'One of this team – and I think most of you know who it is – has lied to you and has lied to me. We are now going to deal with this person.'

Trevor could only find the muddy ground to stare at. He could feel people looking at him, could see his hands trembling, and not just from the cold.

His mind was racing over what could now happen. Only one person could have told Fuller. Any confidence he might have felt towards Martin vanished and he angrily regretted having trusted anybody. He felt sick.

Fuller was speaking. 'Come here, Trevor Huon.'

Trevor remained still.

'Come here!'

As he finally moved, Trevor caught a glimpse of the parents, who were attentively watching and listening to all that was happening. At the edge of the group, with an intrigued look on his face, was Buckley.

Do something, Dad, Trevor thought frantically as he felt Fuller grasp his shoulder. When at last he looked up, it was the team he came face to face with.

'Did you lie to us, Trevor Huon?' Fuller asked in a quiet voice. Trevor said nothing, switching his gaze from the perplexed team to his own muddy shoes.

'Did you?'

'Yes,' Trevor finally answered.

'Have you ever played football before, Huon? Seriously?'

Trevor took a deep breath. 'No.'

'Why then have you been telling us otherwise?'

'I don't know.' It was barely a whisper.

'Speak up!'

'I don't know,' he repeated, stifling the tears that were rising in his eyes, the pain in his throat. Whatever fraction of pride he had left was not going to let him cry in front of everyone.

'Well,' Fuller turned away from Trevor and faced the team. 'So much for our new player.' There was sarcasm in the coach's voice, and he let it occupy another moment of silence.

The team remained in their two even lines, neither moving nor speaking. Their collective faces weren't angry or even mocking, like Fuller's. Instead they were subdued, confused and not entirely sure of what was happening.

Fuller was not yet finished, and he spoke now, crisp and businesslike.

'Well, Under Twelves. What are we going to do with this ... liar? Allow him to remain in disgrace on our team? Letting us down? Or shall we ask him to leave altogether, and just forget it ever happened?'

Fuller's jaw was set, and he seemed to have already made

his own decision. The team looked across uncomfortably at Trevor, looked down at their boots, shot shrugging glances at each other.

'Well?' Fuller asked of them.

Trevor remained perfectly still, eyes cast downward.

'Well?' Fuller demanded again.

At last, someone spoke. 'Let him stay. He's a good runner.' Martin Grace's voice.

Fuller almost shouted. 'What was that?'

'Let him stay,' Martin said once more, his voice muffled by uncertainty. But at that moment, a new voice cut in.

'Just what the hell is going on here?'

Everyone's attention switched from Fuller to Buckley. An angry-faced Buckley, with his cement-dusty boots and his hands on his hips.

'Well? Is this a training session or a court martial?'

'Your son,' Fuller said with sudden politeness, 'has deliberately misled us. I felt it was time his team mates found out. Before it became more of a problem.'

'What d' you mean, "more of a problem"?' Buckley snapped angrily. 'If you couldn't even tell he hadn't played before, I can't see what the problem is!'

'I don't like dishonesty, Mr Huon.'

'Does that mean you make an example of my son like this? Surely there are better ways of dealing with the situation.'

A dull flush spread over Fuller's face. 'Mr Huon, I'll thank you to leave the disciplining of my team to me,' he said through tight lips.

Buckley paused, looking sidelong at the blank faces of the team, and then at Trevor, who had his hands stuffed into his pockets and his gaze still fixed at his feet.

'Well,' Buckley continued, 'since you've chosen to discuss my son's possible shortcomings in front of others, Mr

Fuller, I might just take this opportunity to vent a few of my opinions of you as well.'

Over at the boundary fence the assembled parents, who had been muttering amongst themselves, stopped to listen.

'Firstly,' Buckley continued, 'I think your coaching tactics stink.'

Fuller looked mildly amused. 'Continue, Mr Huon.'

'I don't like the tactics you're teaching these kids. Telling them how to kick the hell out of the other team isn't sport. Neither is it safe. I think you could do well to . . .'

'Mr Huon,' Fuller interrupted, 'I'm training sportsmen here, not pansies. I don't know much about your son, but my team likes to be driven. I teach them aggression because they need it to win.'

'The will to win is one thing. I played league myself once. But aggression in the sense of trying to maim your opponents . . .'

'That might be how it appears to you, Mr Huon. You're a stranger in this town. But I've got a team here that has won every game they've played two years running. They've been playing as a team for four years and I intend to keep them on their winning path. When your son joined, I told him he was a risk. Now that we know he's dishonest, he's even more of a risk. That's my point, Mr Huon.'

Buckley looked at him. 'I'm not saying it wasn't a silly thing for Trevor to do, but it's not sufficient to have him branded as completely dishonest. I know him better than that.'

Fuller shrugged and turned away, no longer interested in the argument. In his usual crisply impatient voice, he informed the team that the day's training session was over.

'Am I to assume,' he said with his back turned to both Trevor and Buckley, 'that Trevor will not be at tomorrow's match?'

'That's Trevor's decision, not mine,' answered Buckley.

Everyone was leaving, the other kids walking over to their waiting parents. Carrying the unused football, Fuller followed them.

Martin Grace straggled at the end of the departing group, occasionally glancing with uncertainty at Buckley and Trevor, who were standing alone on the wet and muddy oval.

Buckley ran a hand through his son's wet hair and said quietly, 'I'll wait for you in the Kombi, eh?'

Trevor nodded.

After a while he stooped to pick up his thick woollen jumper, rain soaked as it was, and put it on. A short distance away, Martin was standing, and Trevor walked across to him.

Martin was looking bemused, open-mouthed as if to say something, but it was Trevor who spoke first.

'You told him,' he said. 'You told Fuller.' Then he turned and walked away. Somehow he still felt uncertain that Martin had told, but there was no other explanation.

Buckley was waiting in the Kombi.

The two of them said nothing on the way home. Once there, Trevor disappeared for a while, walking away for an hour's exploration of the paddocks behind the caravan park. Climbing through wire fences, he negotiated the rain-damp ground with little purpose until it was too dark to see clearly. He made his way grimly back to the Kombi and caravan then, guessing that by now Buckley would have told Kath about training, and that not too much more would have to be explained.

Saying nothing, he slipped into the warmth of the caravan, positioned himself in front of the TV, and tried to watch the usual rerun American cop shows, hoping that this would eliminate the need for talk.

At first nothing was said, although he could sense his parents' glances as they cooked dinner. This was uncomfortable, since Kath and Buckley were frank people, prone to talking out problems as soon as they emerged. But tonight they were strangely silent, as though still deciding how best to talk about all that had happened that day.

'What made you get into that kind of situation, Trev?' his father finally asked.

Trevor, translating that as meaning, 'Why did you do it?' said nothing.

'I didn't realize you'd said all that to them,' Buckley continued.

'I had to,' Trevor answered, embarrassed because the concern just made him feel worse.

'But why?'

'I just did.'

They sat down to dinner. Although hungry, Trevor ate slowly. Kath turned the TV off, substituting one of her cassettes on the portable tape deck.

Against the calmer background of music Buckley said, 'You've played football before, haven't you Trev?'

'Yeah. Just at school.'

'Before this?'

'At other places. Just mucking about in the playground.'

Buckley nodded. 'That's more or less what Kath and I said.'

It took a moment for that remark to sink in, but when it did, Trevor looked up. 'Who did you say that to?'

'One of the parents,' Kath said, 'at last Saturday's match. Don't know whose mum it was, but that's probably how Mr Fuller found out. Sorry.'

Trevor looked down at his plate. 'That's all right. It's not your fault.'

'Might have spared you today's little court martial if we hadn't mentioned it. But we didn't know.'

Trevor didn't reply. There was silence for a minute.

Buckley spoke again. 'Do you like being in the team, Trevor?'

'No. Not really.'

'You going to give it away, then?'

Trevor shook his head.

'Why not?' Buckley asked.

'Because that'd be giving in to Fuller, wouldn't it?' Trevor answered.

Buckley frowned. 'Fuller takes the sport you kids play too seriously. And since we've arrived in this town, he's been giving you a hard time. At school and on the football field.'

'How do you know?' Trevor demanded.

'Because,' his father said patiently, 'I know you well enough to know when you're not happy. And you're not at the moment, are you?'

Trevor avoided his father's gaze. 'No.'

'The logical thing to do then, would be just to forget this whole football thing. Make life easier for yourself.'

Trevor shook his head again. 'I'm not going to give in.'

Buckley and Kath exchanged glances and then watched as Trevor finished eating his meal.

'Did anyone ever tell you, Trevor Huon, that you're as stubborn as hell?' Kath said with a resigned smile. 'What side of the family did you get it from?'

Trevor looked up and almost smiled back. 'Both of you,' he replied.

Nine

Today, it felt worse.

He had told them several times, 'You don't have to come along if you don't want to,' but Kath and Buckley were not to be put off. In the end, he had virtually pleaded with them not to come, but today was the aftermath of the rainsoaked training session and they obviously wanted to show their support for him.

Having guessed by now that his parents were not exactly fanatical about football or Mr Fuller, Trevor had greeted this support with a mixture of thanks and regret. Now he really earnestly wished that they'd stayed at home. He looked around at the gathering crowds, the familiar smattering of parents and grandparents and the kids from school whose faces he recognized.

'Reserve again, today,' Buckley said. It was a statement rather than a question.

Trevor nodded. 'I guess so.'

'If you do get to play,' Buckley added with emphasis, 'be careful, won't you?'

Trevor looked at his father quizzically. 'What d'you mean?'

'You know. Don't get hurt.'

'Jeez, Dad, I've been hurt before. Fallen over things. Fallen off things. Had bleeding noses, black eyes, and all that.'

'I mean, really hurt. Break an arm or a leg or a wrist.

Worse still, your nose. I don't want you looking like someone's hit you in the face with a spade for the rest of your life.'

Trevor groaned. 'You're just trying to put me off!'

'Yes,' said Buckley with a laugh.

'I won't be playing today, anyhow. Probably not for ever, after training.'

His father looked thoughtful.

A familiar voice beside them said, 'Didn't think you'd come along today.' Martin, of course.

Trevor said quickly to Kath and Buckley, 'I'm just going off to find the rest of the team with Martin,' and before they could say anything in reply, he and Martin had walked off into the crowd.

'Didn't think you'd come today,' Martin said again.

Trevor shrugged uncomfortably.

'Why'd you tell me off yesterday, then?'

'I'm sorry.' It took some effort to say this.

'Sorry what?' Martin demanded.

'I thought it was you.'

Martin regarded Trevor with a mixture of antagonism and disdain. 'Me what?'

'Who told Fuller,' Trevor explained lamely, 'about me. I thought it was you.'

Martin rolled his eyes. 'Jeez you're an idiot, Trevor.'

'Well –'

'Why would I do something like that?'

The possibilities were endless. 'I dunno.'

'I'm in enough trouble as it is, sticking up for you. Fuller'll pick on me for the next month. Don't know why I bothered.'

'Why did you then?' Trevor asked, but received no satisfactory answer.

'You're the last one here,' Martin said as they walked on

amongst the sideline crowds. 'That's why we thought you weren't coming.'

The team was assembled in its usual position beside the halfway line. Fuller was nowhere to be seen and, for the moment, the kids engaged in the usual pre-match conversation. Until Martin and Trevor appeared in their midst.

'Hey, here's our number one star,' Brad Clark said loudly. 'Ace footballer Huon.'

'Ace reserve, you mean,' said someone else.

'Ace bull artist.'

They gathered around him, and he waited for the worst.

'Always thought you were lying, Huon.'

'Yeah. We were right all along.'

'Go back to playing soccer, Shorty.'

'Gonna win the game for us today, Huon?'

'Twenty metre dash with the oranges at half-time?'

Laughter.

Trevor endured this in silence, looking occasionally at their reprimanding, you-can't-fool-us faces. But somehow, their rebukes lacked real aggression and soon some of the kids were considering aloud the other things that had brought to an end the previous day's training session.

'Was that your dad, Huon?'

'No, dummy, it was his brother.'

'Bull!'

'He sure looked weird.'

'Like Santa Claus.'

'Santa Claus!'

'He really told Fuller off. Told him where to go.'

'Thought they were gonna start punching into each other.'

'Aw come off it. He's chicken. Like father, like son.'

'Bet you got belted when you got home, eh Huon?'

'No, I didn't,' Trevor answered.

'Bet he's lying again.'

'Come on Trevor, you must have been belted to a pulp.'

'No, I wasn't.'

'Well, what happened?'

'We just talked,' Trevor replied.

'Is that all?'

'Yeah.'

'You're kidding.'

'My dad would've killed me –'

'Yeah, mine too.'

'You gonna leave the team?'

'We don't need you,' sneered Bradley Clark derisively. 'We don't want you.'

'Neither does Fuller,' added someone else. 'He doesn't trust you anyway.'

'So you might as well leave,' concluded another voice.

'Shut up you guys,' Martin Grace said abruptly. 'Trev's not going t' give in just because you tell him to.'

'What's wrong with you all of a sudden, Grace?' Bradley asked loftily. 'Sticking up for Huon all of a sudden.'

'Nothing's wrong, Clark.'

'Huon's gonna quit, aren't you Huon?'

'No,' Trevor said, 'I'm not.'

'We don't need three reserves anyway, Huon. You might as well go home.'

'Why don't you go home, Clark?' Martin said sarcastically. 'Might be quieter round here then.'

Bradley spat meaningfully on the ground. 'You and Huon buddies or something?'

Seeing a few possible meanings for this, the team collapsed into raucous laughter.

Martin raised a fist, gave Bradley a shove with his free hand. 'You wanna go, do you?' he inquired dangerously.

The encircling team started to shout encouragement, but Bradley's angry response was cut short.

'What's going on here?' Fuller demanded.

Everyone stopped to look at the coach, who was flanked by a couple of parents, and strangely enough, no one was willing to offer explanations. Fuller regarded them all sternly before briefly checking the team list.

'Anderson?'

'Here.'

'Barnes?'

'Here.'

'Briggs?'

'Here.'

'Clark?'

'Here.'

'Davies?'

'Here.'

'Evans?'

'Here.'

'Grace?'

'Here.'

Fuller's voice was suddenly stern to the point of anger.

'Huon?'

'Here,' Trev answered, finding Fuller's gaze totally unnerving.

Fuller paused for a moment before continuing.

'Jenkins?'

'Here . . .'

I'm not giving in, Trevor thought quickly to himself, knowing that the coach wanted him nowhere near the football field. The other kids regarded Trevor silently and with puzzlement, knowing full well that he'd be spending today sitting uselessly on the sideline. Just as always.

'Reserves,' Fuller announced, 'Evans, Huon and Grace.'

'How come I'm reserve?' Martin said indignantly.

Fuller ignored him and launched instead into the usual pre-match pep talk. 'Right!' he declared loudly, pointing to an assembled group on the opposite side of the field 'There's your opposition . . .'

Alienated from the content and purpose of Fuller's speech, Trevor lapsed into thought. He looked sideways to Martin, who had his arms angrily folded and was staring at the ground. It was ages since Martin had missed playing a game by being reserve, and he was regarding it not only as Fuller's revenge for the previous day's training, but as an insult. Trevor looked away.

'. . . and who's going to win?' Fuller was shouting.

'CLUB UNDER TWELVES!' the team shouted back.

Under the approving gaze of the cheering parents, the team spilled enthusiastically on to the field.

Jason Evans, Martin Grace and Trevor sat down more or less where they'd been standing, in the usual position next to the bucket of half-time oranges.

'How come you're reserve?' Jason asked Martin.

'Prob'ly because of sticking up for Trev at training yesterday.'

'Oh. Yeah.'

'Because he was too dumb to stick up for himself.'

Trevor shot Martin a look, as the referee's whistle commenced the game. With a thud, the ball was kicked into flight, and the two teams exploded into motion across the field.

'I mean,' Martin added, more out of anger for having forfeited a game than at Trevor, 'you never say anything. All you do is listen and take what people sling at you.' Then he added, 'Anyway, you'll never get to play, now. Prob'ly made things worse for yourself than before.'

They silently watched the first few minutes of play. Beside them were the parents yelling frenzied encouragement, and somewhere in the barracking melee was Fuller yelling advice.

'Pass that ball out . . .!'

The minutes passed.

Trevor stood up quickly and surveyed the noisy crowd around him. To one side he could see Kath and Buckley talking to each other and not paying much attention to the game. He started to walk in the opposite direction.

'Where're you going?' Martin asked.

'Just for a walk,' Trevor replied. 'No use staying here.'

'You'll get into trouble,' Jason Evans warned. 'Fuller'll kill you.'

Ignoring these remarks Trevor walked off into the crowd, scuffing the expendable football boots over the foot-worn ground. Around him the game and the noise progressed, but he made the effort to cut himself off from it all, to dwell instead on thoughts of being a reserve for the rest of his days. He thought again about Martin unpredictably defending him at training, and briefly felt sorry that he had had to miss a game because of it. Why exactly Martin had said anything at all puzzled Trevor. It had been a bit of a shock hearing Martin's bullying cynicism temporarily replaced by disguised kindness. Martin had been treading the line between remaining faithful to the kids he'd grown up with, and being tentative friends with a newcomer. Which made things unpredictable.

But then, Martin was a misfit of sorts too, being almost a year older than the other kids. The age gap alone set him a little apart from the team at least, and it always appeared to be a slight struggle for him to stay in favour with them. Intuition allowed Trevor to sort this much out for himself, and it was only then that his own stubbornness really dawned on him. Membership of the team had developed into a half-crazy essential, though he realized that he'd never get beyond being a reserve on the sideline.

But I'm not giving in, he told himself again, and directed the comment silently to Fuller, the team and surrounding parents alike.

The noise around him rose and fell. He walked past the groups of parents, but suddenly came to a halt as a conversation nearby caught his hearing.

'. . . and apparently he'd never played football before.'

'Yes, so I heard.'

Two of the parents stood amid the sideline crowd, their backs to Trevor. He couldn't tell whose mothers they were. They were both dressed awkwardly in fashion slacks and jumpers, and in reluctant command of a couple of noisy young children. They talked on, and as he listened it became abundantly clear who it was they were discussing.

'Were you here yesterday, when the father turned up and started causing trouble?'

'Yes, wasn't it terrible? As for the hair and beard on him . . .'

'Looked like something out of the stone age.'

'And the child doesn't look much better either. Hard to tell whether he was a boy or a girl at first. And the things he wears at school!'

With rising indignation, Trevor kept listening.

'. . . no school uniform apparently. The parents probably can't afford it.'

'Yes, from what I've heard they're seasonal workers, you know, no fixed address . . .'

'Terrible.'

'The husband's bricklaying on the extensions down at the club.'

'Have you seen the mother, though?'

'No.'

'Oh, she's in town a fair bit. Dresses like a gypsy. Couldn't begin to imagine when she's washed her hair last.'

'Well they don't seem to these days anyway, do they?'

'Oh, this lot are living down in the caravan park. Seems that all they do is move from place to place. Very unsettling for the child. He's bound to end up illiterate like the parents probably are.'

'But I can't get over how the boy got into the team in the first place. It's very bad for the other boys. We're hoping to come through undefeated again this year.'

'Yes, of course.'

The next comment identified one of the women as Martin Grace's mum.

'. . . yes. I'm still angry about Martin missing today's game.'

'Yes, he is a good player.'

'Mr Fuller's put him on reserve. It seems to be because of the Huon boy.'

At this point, Mrs Grace turned around. Unprepared for whom she came face to face with, her mouth opened to say something more, but she abruptly turned away, the words unsaid. Trevor glowered at them both, longing to say something appropriately abusive, but nothing suitable would come to mind. He could see Mrs Grace murmuring quickly to the other mother, who likewise turned around to give Trevor a brief, shocked stare.

Trevor's mind was an angry confusion and he stood there for a moment longer, trying to think of something to say. At last he didn't say anything, instead giving the mothers a rude hand signal that they didn't see, before heading back to where he had been sitting with Martin and Jason.

'What's wrong with you?' Martin asked when he saw the obvious anger on Trevor's face.

'Nothing,' Trevor answered sullenly.

'Sure looks like something's wrong.'

'Nothing's wrong,' Trevor repeated loudly and impatiently. 'Why don't you shut up and leave me alone?'

Martin's offhand concern ground to a halt. Surprised at the outburst, he said nothing more for the time being.

Things on the football field didn't seem to be progressing too well, either. When the half-time whistle blew, the team trooped tiredly from the field, to be immediately berated by Fuller.

'What's wrong with you guys?' the coach demanded. The team offered no response and concentrated grimly on eating oranges and getting their collective breath back before the second half.

'Those blokes over there think they've got you beat.' Fuller continued, 'What a joke! I want you all moving up much quicker when they play the ball. Knock them over and put them on the ground, hard. Let them know when they're tackled. I want them scared of you and only half watching what they're doing so that they start making mistakes. That's when *we* start scoring the points. You, O'Leary – have you fallen in love with the football or something?'

'No sir.'

'Well pass it out, then!' the coach shouted angrily. 'You're in a team, son, there's more than one of you . . .'

The parents stood around and listened approvingly. Afterwards, they would offer their own tactical advice on how to immobilize the kids in the opposing team. Fuller's mid-match tirade continued unabated.

'. . . and I want you back on that field playing like champs. I want to see that ball being passed out. I want to see quick, aggressive tackling and I want to see points scored. Is that clear?'

Subdued, the team nodded.

'I couldn't hear you,' Fuller said at a half-shout. 'Is that clear?'

'YES!' they shouted back.

'Right,' Fuller went on, 'because I've a bargain to put to you.'

The kids all stopped to listen.

'If you can win this game with at least a five-point margin, you've got yourselves a free night at the movies in town this evening.'

This was greeted by shrill cheers.

'But only if you win!' shouted Fuller emphatically. 'Right?'

'RIGHT!'

They had been bargained with before, and it had almost always proved to be a successful tactic of encouragement. Today, it looked like succeeding again. As the game progressed into the second half, Fuller's team slowly improved their hold over the opposing side. They scored, converted, scored again. Each set of gained points was nicely accounted for by bursts of cheering from the sidelines and Fuller, striding backwards and forwards, spearheaded the applause with his continual shouted advice.

The three reserves watched in relative silence.

'They're gonna win this,' said Jason Evans at last, 'I can tell.'

Martin nodded. 'Yeah. For sure.'

Trevor said nothing.

Martin looked at him. 'What's wrong with you?' he asked again.

Trevor grimaced. 'Nothing.'

'Well you've got the poohs about something.'

Seeing that Trevor seemed to be in no mood for talk, Martin stopped to think about something for a few moments. Eventually he stood up.

'I'm just going for a walk,' he announced.

Ever cautious, Jason reminded him, 'You'll get it off Fuller if he sees you walking around.'

'Aw, Fuller can go jump!' replied Martin, and walked off.

He was gone for a good ten minutes, leaving Jason to worry about the consequences and Trevor to recall again the conversation he'd overheard. The two mothers' remarks were still fresh in his mind, the insinuations that Buckley and Kath were no-hopers, and worse. He was glad his parents hadn't heard it all.

Martin came back. 'Hey, Trev!'

'What?'

'You want to come round to my place this arvo?'

Trevor was incredulous. 'What was that?'

'I said, do you want to come round to my place this arvo? After the game?'

'What for?'

'For a visit of course, stupid,' replied Martin impatiently, 'and then to stay for dinner, and for the night, you know! Looks like we'll be going to the pictures tonight. We're gonna win this game for sure.'

'Whose idea was this?' Trevor asked suspiciously, immediately thinking of the talkative Mrs Grace.

'Mine, of course,' said Martin. 'Whose did you think?'

Trevor shrugged.

'Well?' insisted Martin. 'D' you want to come around. Will your parents mind?'

Trevor shook his head. 'No, it'll be all right ...' He couldn't see any polite way to get out of the visit, and quickly decided to endure whatever might eventuate as far as Mrs Grace and her opinions of him were concerned. 'Okay,' he said, 'I'll come around. What time?'

'Come round at four,' said Martin, and satisfied, sat down once more to watch the concluding stages of the football match.

Ten

Came four o'clock.

Apprehensively, Trevor walked the distance from the caravan park to Martin Grace's house in the middle of the town. The Saturday afternoon was concluding quietly, and he savoured the stillness around him, felt the movement only of the slightly stirring breeze against his face. He walked past shops empty of people save for the travelling population that haunted the takeaway counter of the milkbar.

'You'd better pretend to be civilized,' Kath had told him before he'd left, instructing him to take pyjamas if he was still intending staying the night at Martin's. These were in the patchwork bag he had hitched over one shoulder, along with his toothbrush. In the pocket of his homemade overalls was some spending money from his father.

'For ice-cream and Jaffas,' Buckley had said generously, determined that the free evening at the movies was to be enjoyed.

For himself, Trevor felt nothing but determination to prove Mrs Grace wrong.

He found the house in one of the streets behind the shopping centre. Momentarily he hesitated at the front gate, long enough to survey the meticulously tidy garden that surrounded the ageing but equally meticulous house. It was a world away from the Kombi and the caravan. Slowly he entered the gateway.

Martin lurked behind a screen door. 'You're here at last!' he said with a note of impatience. 'I thought your parents would've given you a lift or something.'

'No,' Trevor said, 'I wanted to walk, anyway.'

Martin shrugged. 'Oh well ... wipe your feet, anyway. Mum'll go off her brain if you walk dirt into the house.'

He followed Martin up a shadowy carpeted hallway.

She was in the kitchen cooking, and stopped to regard him uncomfortably. She was tall and stocky like Martin. Trying to control the sense of hostility in him, Trevor looked expressionlessly at her face, shiny with cosmetics. 'Hullo Mrs Grace,' he said in a monotone.

'Hullo Trevor,' she said with equal flatness. 'Glad to have you around.'

He stared around at the crisply renovated kitchen, the bright cafe-window curtains above the sink, the matching cupboards, the monolithic refrigerator, the seemingly endless array of plastic and china knick-knacks and tourist souvenirs that occupied window sills and cupboard tops.

'A bit different to a caravan, I would imagine,' she said pointedly.

'Yes,' Trevor answered, 'a bit bigger.'

Manners satisfied, the two boys went back up the hall, heading for the safety of Martin's bedroom. Carpet – there was carpet everywhere. Half of what he saw looked too sacred to tread on, and he began to feel as though he was in a museum and not somebody's house. The lounge-room furniture was starkly modern. It was the sort of furniture Kath and Buckley would probably have said rude things about. Trevor tried to imagine their reaction to all this; to the size, brightness and sheer look of affluence about the house.

'Those're my sisters,' Martin said, pointing to a row of

87

wedding photos hanging on a wall. 'They've all got kids now.' Then he added proudly, 'I'm an uncle.'

'Are you the youngest?' Trevor asked tentatively, looking up also at the prints of galloping horses that hung on the same wall.

'Yeah,' Martin answered. 'Are you?'

'There's only me.'

'Oh. What about cousins?'

'Most of them live around Sydney. We usually go to visit them at Christmas time.'

'Jeez, that'd be good. Most of mine live round here, and you see them all year long. Gets a bit boring. You know Michael O'Leary?'

'Yeah.'

'Well he's one of my cousins. Didn't know that, eh?'

Martin's room was a menagerie of objects. Model planes were displayed along cupboard tops and window sills. Football team posters hung around the walls, photos of cars and motorcycles, and there was a religious picture above the bed. And spread along another wall, sports pennants. *200 metres freestyle, Martin Grace. 200 metres backstroke, Martin Grace. Best and fairest, Martin Grace. Most improved player, Martin Grace.* On a wooden chest of drawers, there was a row of sporting trophies. *Under 8s finalists, Under 10s undefeated, Under 11s undefeated.*

A sort of clinical tidiness governed the room. One corner was occupied by a folding bed that was obviously for Trevor.

'What d' you think?' Martin asked, indicating the entire room.

'It's great,' Trevor said, comparing it unfavourably with his own bedroom.

'D' you have a room of your own in the caravan ...?'

Martin started to ask, but then corrected himself. 'No, wait. You've got your bedroom in the Kombi.'

'Yeah.'

'What's that like?'

'It's okay. Bit cramped.'

'I reckon it'd be great.'

Every so often, Trevor was aware of Mrs Grace's presence and several times looked to see her hovering in the background or peering around doorways, seemingly checking up on things. He waited till she was out of earshot. Interested in how Martin would react, Trevor asked bluntly, 'Your mother doesn't like me, does she?'

Martin appeared surprised. 'She thinks you're all right, I guess. She always goes a bit off her head when other kids are around, you know, in case they break something. Don't worry about it.'

Trevor, who knew otherwise, wasn't convinced. He could picture Mrs Grace in her kitchen, frowning about his being in the same house. The disapproval was not going to change in the course of one afternoon, and he knew it.

'Hey, what about winning the match eighteen to seven. Pretty good, eh?'

'Yeah,' Trevor answered. 'Great.'

'Just as long as Fuller lets me play next week.'

'Has he shouted the team to the movies before?'

'Yeah. Not very often, but. The club pays for it anyway, not Fuller, so it's not as though he's being super-generous to us.'

'What happens when he sees me at the theatre too, though?'

Martin shrugged. 'What can he say? You're still in the team, even if you are a measly reserve. And besides, he knows if he says anything that your dad'll tell him off.'

A room at the back of the house contained a pool table.

'You know how to play?' Martin asked.

'Yeah, sure,' replied Trevor, starting to extract the coloured balls from the corner pockets and arranging them on the table's felt surface.

Martin did the same. 'Where'd you learn?'

'Ages ago, when I was little.'

'You are now.'

'When I was younger,' Trevor said reproachfully.

'But where?'

'All over the place . . .' Ages ago that had been, Buckley teaching him the rudiments of pool and snooker in the back rooms of rural hotels. So long ago it was, that he remembered being barely able to see over the top of the table. 'My dad taught me.'

'Yeah, so'd mine.'

'What does your dad do?'

'Runs the real estate place in town. He's off somewhere working this arvo. What about your dad?'

'Everything. Fruitpicking, welding –'

'Bricklaying.'

'Bricklaying, fixes cars and all that.'

'Jeez, he knows a lot.'

'Yeah.'

'What's it like, but? Moving around all the time?'

'It's good.'

'I reckon I'd hate it.'

'You get used to it.'

'But have you always been doing that?'

Trevor shook his head. 'Not always. We used to live in a house.'

'What happened?'

'It's my grandmother's house. We used to all live there. Then my grandmother decided to move to the city and once she'd gone and didn't need us for company any more, my parents thought they'd take the chance to do what they'd always wanted, and do a bit of travelling.'

'Is there anyone living there now?'

'People rent it, sometimes for holidays.'

'Oh,' Martin said, and gave Trevor a cue stick. 'Let's see how good you can play.'

They played pool, several times over. Trevor was trying to engross himself in what he was doing, but his thoughts were very much elsewhere. Being inside a house such as this awoke distant images of the house he had once lived in himself, and morosely he felt out of place. Occasionally he considered with some surprise how friendly Martin was being, but even this extraordinary circumstance didn't help much. He started to wish he was back home in the caravan, so he could put aside the facade of enjoying himself and of being resilient to the critical glances of Mrs Grace.

He sat uncomfortably at the dinner table that evening with Martin next to him and Mr and Mrs Grace facing him from the opposite side of the tablecloth. Sombrely, he employed his best table manners and refrained from commenting that he wasn't all that keen on eating meat. Mr Grace, in business shirt and nightmare tie, asked him lots of questions.

'So what does your father do, Trevor?'

Trevor told him more or less what he'd told Martin.

'And what about your mother?'

'She used to be a teacher.'

'Oh?'

'She gave it away when I was born, though. Sometimes she fruitpicks with Dad and sometimes she makes clothes to sell. Like the ones I'm wearing.' He looked at Mrs Grace.

She returned the look and replied, 'Yes, I thought they might have been.'

Mr Grace's talking and questioning continued relentlessly. 'Yes, we've seen your Kombivan around town. Smart machine; it looks as though it's been to a fair few places.'

'Yes it has,' Trevor replied.

'And how do you like moving about from town to town?'

Trevor groaned inwardly.

'I mean, do you mind going to a new school every few months?' The man's questions were politely earnest but pointless.

'No,' Trevor replied obstinately, 'I don't mind moving around. I like it.'

'And how are you finding football? Enjoying it?'

'Yeah. It's great.'

'Yes,' continued Mr Grace with a smile, 'Martin's going to keep playing for the club. We're rather hoping he'll take it up professionally one day. Right, Martin?'

'Yeah,' Martin said, without much enthusiasm.

Apart from the more or less compulsory replies he had to make, Trevor said nothing. He was aware of Martin's mum's steady gaze that seemed to be evaluating his every move. She seemed to be waiting for him to commit some breach of etiquette that for her would have typified his caravan park origins. Carefully, he avoided replying with his mouth full and dropping food on the shag pile carpet. They watched the usual smattering of news-time television until it was time to leave for the movies.

'I wish they'd quit going on about football,' Martin said as the two of them walked along the town's darkening streets. 'I'm getting sick of football, anyway.'

'Are you?' Trevor was surprised.

Martin didn't reply directly. 'Anyway,' he said at last, 'I'm glad you're staying at my place tonight. Bit of a change from having to talk to some dumb cousin.'

The theatre was alive with activity. A blaze of neon lights

contrasting brilliantly with the darkness of the evening threw light on to the people that crowded the steps and the foyer. Out on the street, cars drove back and forth, searching for the convenient parking spaces that were fast disappearing. The crowd was mostly the local kids, a few parents, a lot of teenagers and a few strange people that were obviously tourists. A good double feature in the small town always attracted a crowd, and tonight was no exception.

The team had grouped together in the foyer, and were busy eyeing the tourists, calling out to other kids they knew, and speculating about the evening's movie.

'Should be a scary one.'

'You reckon?'

'Lots of blood and guts –'

'Shooting –'

'. . . and some dumb Bugs Bunny cartoon on first.'

'Who's got the tickets?'

'Whose, ours?'

'Yeah.'

'Bradley's got them. He's in charge of them.'

'Who said?'

'Mr Fuller.'

'Where's Mr Fuller?'

'He's not here, stupid. He never comes along, you know that.'

'Prob'ly down at the club.'

'Prob'ly.'

Trevor meanwhile had ducked off to the theatre kiosk to put the money Buckley had given him to practical use. Presently he returned to the foyer clutching a box of Jaffas.

'Well, c'mon Brad,' Jason said impatiently, 'hand the tickets out. They're not all yours, y' know.'

'Okay, okay, don't get your knickers in a knot ...'

93

Bradley dealt out to the clamouring team with maddening slowness.

'Where's mine?' Trevor asked hesitantly, when it seemed that everyone else except him had received a ticket.

Brad looked at him seriously for a moment. 'Hey, the midget reserve's here,' he said in a loud jesting voice. 'Didn't get a ticket for you, Huon. Guess you'll have to go home.'

A few of the kids laughed. Brad mimicked Trevor's dumbfounded face, before holding a ticket up. 'Ha, sucked in again, Huon,' he said, and threw the ticket in the air for Trevor to catch. At that moment, the foyer lights dimmed around them. They stampeded into the black vastness of the theatre with the rest of the crowd.

The usherette, a fierce woman wielding a powerful water-proof torch, occasionally interrupted the darkness inside the theatre by shining the torch across the audience in search of troublemakers. During the course of the evening she kicked several out, although a couple of these employed commando tactics and successfully crawled back to their seats. And when it seemed the theatre was getting a bit stuffy, the usherette climbed the stairs to the rear of the theatre and opened the louvre windows. Battalions of mosquitoes were carried in on an arctic breeze.

Protests rang out in the darkness.

'Who opened the bloody windows?'

'Yeah, we're freezing down here in the stalls.'

The waterproof torch flashed on and scanned the theatre. There was instant quiet, and the movie laboured on. Somebody rolled an empty drink can down the aisle steps into the stalls at the front, and occasionally, paper missiles whizzed through the darkness. A deep voice in the dress circle provided a very uncensored commentary on what the movie stars could have been saying, but weren't. There were bursts of appreciative laughter, until the usherette's torchlight silenced the audience once more.

The team sat in a group in the stalls, along with a multitude of other locals. Apart from Michael O'Leary being threatened with expulsion, the kids managed miraculously to escape the wrath of the usherette, an elderly lady who claimed to know the local children better than their parents did. At a strategic point in the movie, Trevor opened his box of Jaffas and greedily ate three or four in one mouthful. It didn't take long for Martin, who was next to him, to detect the location of the sweets.

'Hey,' he whispered to Trevor, 'how's about giving us one?'

Trevor shrugged, and handed him the box.

'Only one, but.'

Martin said loudly, 'Who wants a Jaffa?'

The response was immediate, and before Trevor could retrieve the box, it had disappeared down along the row.

'Jeez, thanks Martin.'

'Yeah, thanks.'

A few other appreciative voices were heard.

'They weren't mine, they were Trevor's,' said Martin.

'Gee, thanks, Huon. You're really generous.'

'Yeah, thanks.'

The usherette's torch flashed on, and the kids' silence resumed.

'You're a rat, Martin,' Trevor eventually whispered angrily as the Jaffa box was returned to him, empty.

'What?' Martin whispered back.

'I said, you're a rat. That was really low.'

'Aw, stop being a sook, Huon. Jeez you're a baby sometimes.'

On the theatre screen another cowboy died. The audience cheered appreciatively, the usherette's torch flashed on yet again, another drink can rolled down the aisle, and someone burped very loudly.

Trevor meanwhile watched the movie blankly, and decided that he wasn't enjoying it at all. He started thinking instead about how he could avoid staying the night at Martin's.

When the lights came on at interval he walked outside in the midst of the jostling crowd. He successfully separated himself from the rest of the team, who all seemed intent on getting themselves a prime position at the counter of the theatre kiosk, and stood for a while by himself near the theatre entrance. It was taking a little time to decide just what to do.

Unnoticed, he slowly moved away from the general crowd and walked further and further from the theatre's dazzle until he was in the dimmed light of the deserted shopping centre. Then he ran for a short distance, his footsteps echoing hollowly on the cement footpath, past the shop-fronts, past the service station into the tranquil chill of the evening. Eventually his run broke to a walk and he made the effort then to walk slowly, ambling along the outlying streets to the caravan park.

He found walking in the darkness surprisingly pleasant, because the town assumed a completely different mood at night. The Norfolk pines swished eerily in the breeze, the houses cast their light through curtain-covered windows. Looming behind the town was the shadow of the mountains and above, the stars and the gathering mist.

He worked now over the consequences of arriving unexpectedly at the caravan park, and wondered what Kath and Buckley might say. Whatever their response, he felt almost sure that leaving the theatre had been the right thing for him to do. The day's football match and Mrs Grace's comments still rang clearly in his mind.

Abruptly, the day's experiences began forming themselves into words and sentences in his mind. He came to the neon-lit entrance of the caravan park, resolving to write it all down, somehow.

The lights in the caravan were still on, and faintly he could hear Kath and Buckley playing their guitars and singing songs.

Just then, he remembered that he'd left his shoulderbag back at Martin Grace's.

Eleven

'I think an apology's in order, Trev.'

'Well his mother wasn't very nice. She's the main reason I didn't stay.'

'What do you mean, "not very nice"?'

'Well she, um . . . I dunno. Just the way she spoke to me.'

Kath sighed. 'Well I wasn't there so I won't enter into that particular discussion. But apologize to Martin, at least.'

'Oh Mum!'

'I mean, it's not very nice leaving your friend in the lurch like that. You were invited to stay, after all.'

'I'm not sure he is my friend.'

'Trevor!'

'All right,' he sighed, 'I'll apologize.'

He walked off then and sulked for a while, feeling angry, feeling that he was right and that Kath, for once, was wrong. The more he thought about it, the more he felt that not staying at Martin's had been the only thing to do. Mrs Grace's hostility was still fresh in his mind, subtly expressed as it might have been. The way she had watched him, the things she had said . . . or had she really? For a moment he thought he could have imagined it, but then uncomfortably remembered what he had heard Mrs Grace saying about Kath and Buckley at the football match.

I didn't imagine it, he thought with some decisiveness, *she really thinks we're no good.* Sure of it now, he glared around the caravan park, hating the coloured lights between the trees, dull now, in the morning sunshine, and the untidy clutter of vehicles and buildings. His mind moved to familiar thoughts about being somewhere else.

'G'day Trev,' said a voice beside him.

Trevor frowned, turning to look at Martin.

'You left your bag behind,' Martin said when Trevor remained silent. 'I brought it back for you.' He held up the patchwork shoulderbag.

'Thanks,' Trevor replied without much enthusiasm.

'Thought you might need it back, eh?'

'Yeah.'

'Where're you going?' Martin had to run a few steps to catch up with Trevor, who was striding back to the caravan.

'Just to put my bag away,' Trevor replied. Once at his own campsite, he ducked into the annexe and threw the bag into the back of the Kombi.

'So this is where you live,' Martin said with some interest, peering about at the caravan, Kombi and array of family possessions. 'Jeez, is that your surfboard?'

Trevor walked outside again. 'Surprised your mother let you come around here,' he said with some sarcasm.

'How come you're in such a bad mood?' Martin asked.

Trevor shrugged. 'I'm not in a bad mood. I just wondered.'

'Then how come you racked off last night?'

They were standing a short distance from the caravan and Kombi now, Trevor with his hands in his jeans pockets and his eyes fixed on the ground, Martin shifting his weight from foot to foot, restlessly trying to make some sense of everything.

'Well?' Martin asked. 'How come you didn't stay?'

For a moment, it was hard not to lump Martin in with Mrs Grace, and Trevor was about to launch into his earlier

99

thoughts about unfairness when he heard a rapping noise at one of the caravan windows. He looked up to see Kath's face behind the glass, frowning and pointing at Martin. This particular sign language Trevor read as meaning, 'Apologize!' – as if he needed further reminders.

'What does your mother want?'

'Nothing,' Trevor answered and flashed Martin a glance. 'I'm sorry about leaving last night.'

'Then how come you did?' Martin asked belligerently, more interested in explanations than apologies.

'I just did.'

'Jeez, you're slack.'

'I'm not.'

'You are. My parents weren't real pleased.'

'Well that's their bad luck.'

'See? You're just slack.'

'I'm not. There were special reasons.'

'Huh!'

Trevor turned and walked away, heading towards the fringe of trees and the steel-framed playground equipment.

'See?' Martin called after him. 'You're just weak. Can't take anything anyone says about you. I try to be your friend and this is what I get.' He watched as Trevor sat down on one of the swings and stared stonily into space. 'Bloody sissy!' Martin added for good measure, remaining where he'd stopped for a while longer, pondering over the stupidity of some people. But eventually he walked over and sat down on the swing next to Trevor.

There was a moment's silence.

'If you're trying to be my friend,' Trevor said, kicking one foot in the dust, 'how come you give me such a hard time?'

'I don't!' Martin protested. 'You just can't take the things I say. Haven't you ever had friends who have goes at you?'

'No.'

Martin sighed. 'No wonder you're so soft. Like Fuller says –'

'Fuller's an idiot. Even you said that.'

'Like Fuller says, one day you'll turn into a girl.'

'He's hung up if he thinks that's the worst insult. At least the girls don't go round trying to prove they're better than each other, like you guys on the footy team do.'

'You're on the team, too.'

'So what?'

'So how come you wanted to play in the first place?'

'To prove I wasn't as stupid as you all thought I was.'

'Huh.'

'You think I'm stupid.'

'I think you're a nut case,' said Martin, and laughed.

Trevor knew that he was still being stirred, but decided he was sick of the argument and wanted it over and done with.

'I dunno why you even bother turning up for training and for games,' Martin said. 'Fuller'll never let you play.'

'I know that.'

'He just doesn't trust you. Especially after finding out you never played before.'

Trevor nodded.

'If I were you, I'd give up. Forget about it. You've had heaps off everyone already.'

'I don't want to give up.'

Martin rolled his eyes in mild exasperation as Trevor started absently pushing backwards and forwards on the swing.

'You'll never get to play a single game,' Martin continued, but with a brooding sort of note to his voice. 'Didn't do any good sticking up for you in the first place.'

Trevor kept swinging, backwards and forwards, backwards and forwards.

'I've got an idea,' Martin said at last.

Trevor brought the swing to a squeaking halt. 'What did you say?'

'An idea. To get you to play.' Seeing a faint glimmer of mistrust on Trevor's face, Martin hastily added, 'I'm serious.'

'What sort of idea?'

'You really want to play, don't you?'

'Yeah. I guess so.'

'Okay. We've got three reserves. You, Andrew and Jason. Right?'

'Right.'

'Well, if two kids on the field get hurt, two of the reserves go on to replace them. If another kid who's on the field gets hurt, the third reserve – that's you – has to go on.'

'That's mad,' Trevor grimaced. 'What if three kids don't get hurt?'

'They don't get hurt at all,' said Martin with a grin, 'because they'll be pretending.'

'It won't work,' said Trevor with finality.

'Well, you think of a better idea then,' answered Martin.

As always, Martin was persistent.

By Tuesday or Wednesday he had seemingly forgotten about arguing with Trevor over the weekend and was now convinced that his scheme was going to work.

'I've talked to some of the other kids,' he told Trevor, 'and they said they'll be in it.'

'They'd better be good actors, then,' Trevor said with some apprehension. 'Pretending they've been injured.'

'You'll have to be a good actor, too. Pretending you can play.' When Trevor looked offended, Martin added, 'Well, we know you can play. But you know what I mean . . .'

'Yeah. Sure.' The more Trevor thought about the idea, the more it seemed that it would never work.

'Your big chance,' Martin kept reminding him.

Sitting in the classroom, surrounded by the other kids bent over comprehension exercises, Trevor dwelt on the absurdity of other kids pretending to be injured on a football field, just so that he could go out there and prove to someone that he was capable of chasing after a ball. It was a crazy idea, but slowly he convinced himself that it was going to happen and that it had to work.

'Stand up, Trevor Huon.'

Surprised out of daydreaming, Trevor duly pushed his chair back and stood beside his desk.

Mr Fuller solemnly held up a familiar exercise book. 'Know what this is, Trevor Huon?'

'My writing book,' Trevor replied without expression, 'sir.'

'Exactly. And if I were you, I wouldn't be proud of it.'

The rest of the class had started to divert their attention from comprehension exercises, but a reprimanding glance from the teacher caused faces to be pointed at desks once more.

'The writing, as usual, needs improvement,' Mr Fuller continued, 'and so does your story. Why is it, Huon, that everyone in the room seems to have imagination, but you don't?'

'I don't know.'

The teacher's casual brand of sarcasm showed on his face, which displayed neither anger nor a smile, merely a calculating look that Trevor found uncomfortable to face. Mr Fuller shook the exercise book for emphasis. 'I asked everyone in the class to write an imaginary story. Do you know what that means?'

'Something made up.'

'Sir!'

'Sir.'

'Exactly. Why then did you choose to write an auto-biography? Everyone else seemed capable of imagination. They made up their stories. Why not you?'

'Don't know, sir.'

'I don't particularly want to read about your life story, colourful as it may be.' The teacher paused. 'You've got less than a week to finish this project. Because you did the wrong thing in the first place, you're running out of time. By next Monday, I want to see this exercise book with a new story in it. Finished. Understand?'

'Yes sir,' Trevor answered, feeling the resentment rising.

'Here is your book. Come and collect it.'

Trevor walked hesitantly to the teacher's desk and picked the offending exercise book up from where it had been disdainfully placed. As he turned to return to the relative safety and distance of the chair next to Martin, the teacher said, 'Remember, Huon. A new story, finished by next Monday. And before you sit down . . .'

The other kids once more seemed to have abandoned their work, and had fixed their surreptitious attention on Trevor and the irritated teacher.

'Why is it, Trevor Huon, that you never see fit to wear appropriate school clothing?'

Trevor looked down at what he was wearing.

'Why do we have to put up with the sight of you in sandals, jeans – usually patched – and hair that constantly looks untidy, mainly because it needs cutting?'

Shut up, you cretin, Trevor thought to himself and aloud, said, 'I don't know, sir,' not so much to the teacher as to the floor.

'Neither do I. I suppose it's too much to hope that you will deign to appear in proper school clothing, but it would be appreciated if you could wear decent shoes and socks, like the rest of us. Now sit down.'

Sure that his face was scarlet with the anger and frustration he felt, Trevor made an effort to resume the comprehension work. He wrote erratically for the next few minutes until Mr Fuller stood up and left the classroom for the office next door. Briefly he flicked open the writing book, long enough to take in the mass of red biro lines and comments that covered his incomplete story. Without stopping to read the teacher's comments, he slowly closed the book.

'What are you gonna do now?' one of the other kids asked.

'Buy a new book,' Trevor replied.

'And make up a new story?'

'No.' He paused, and then added. 'Write the same one out again, and finish it.'

'You're mad,' said Angela Simmons, and a few others agreed.

'Fuller'll really go off his brain.'

'He'll give you an even harder time.'

Trevor shrugged, his mind made up.

Martin looked at him sympathetically. 'He's a bastard, isn't he?'

'You bet.'

'That's why,' Martin continued, 'you have to play in the game on Sunday.'

The days were like a countdown.

'Get those legs going!' Fuller shouted from the sidelines at Friday training. 'I want running, not a waltz!'

With their usual numb persistence, the team sprinted across the field in a broad row. At one end, Martin Grace ran with the ball.

'Right!' Fuller shouted, 'Pass that ball out! Straight and fast.'

Martin shot the ball sideways to Jason. Jason passed it on to Bradley, Bradley to Tony, Tony to Trevor, Trevor to David, and on to the end of the line.

'Stop!' Fuller shouted. 'Start again. Huon, you pass that ball, boy! You're not handing out lollies. Or haven't I told you before? Pass the ball properly, or go home. And that goes for the rest of you, too. Your performance is pathetic. It's fortunate the game is on Sunday, this week – you can all turn up for an extra training session tomorrow.'

Groaning, the line of kids re-formed, started running once more.

Despite some encouraging looks from Martin, Trevor fumed silently. *I did so pass it properly*, he thought as he caught the football and swung it on to the kid next to him. *I'm just as good as the other kids*.

At home in the caravan that night, he stared ruefully at his written story in the exercise book and at the contemptuous comments written by Mr Fuller.

'What are you working on?' asked Buckley, who was washing up.

'My story,' Trevor replied, and opened a new exercise book to the first page, placing it on the table in front of him.

'Oh. I see.'

He looked at the two books for a long time. He decided that the story lacked the right sort of beginning, so he spent some time in thought. Over on her bed, Kath was writing letters and Buckley whistled softly to himself over the dishes. Taking advantage of the relative quietness, Trevor mentally sifted through time past for an appropriate early memory with which to begin the story. At first, the right words didn't appear in his mind and seemingly refused to. There were the familiar pictures of caravan parks, of a dozen different country towns and as many schools. He'd already written that down.

And then he remembered them: photos in an album, of him before he'd even started school. These photographs reminded him of his memories of sand and ocean, of the house he'd once lived in. He couldn't remember its exact form or location, just some impressions of the rooms inside. A bright sunny kitchen and grass-matted lounge-room were the parts he best remembered.

He looked at his parents, with the intention of saying something. But it was a long time since he'd asked them directly about the beach and the house, and for some reason he felt uneasy about asking now.

So he looked back at his exercise books. Slowly, the words came together, and he picked up his pen and started to write.

Twelve

The sky had clouded impressively for the day.

Overnight, it had rained. The greyness was complete; a blanket of haze subdued the town and the surrounding forested and grazing hills to a cool stillness, punctuated only by the vivid green of the Norfolk pines and the small-town backyards.

Today, the noise at the football ground seemed more intense than usual. Trevor stared vacantly across the patchy stretch of ground, feeling threatened, trying to come to terms with things to come. Today it was actually going to happen. He was going to play. Martin's crazy plan was going to subvert Fuller's iron-hard rule on the team. The idea had blossomed into a conspiracy, mainly because Martin had employed his height and strength to convince the other kids it was a good idea.

They huddled together in a furtive group on the sidelines, discussing and verbally rehearsing what was to happen.

'– and then get caught in one of the tackles, Dave.'

'Go under and make it look as though you've been kicked.'

'But don't all get injured at once. If we all go off in the first half, Fuller'll spring us for sure.'

'You guys are nuts,' said the ever-pessimistic Bradley Clark. 'Anyway, I'm dobbing you in to Fuller.'

'You do, Clark,' warned Martin Grace, 'and I'll smack your teeth in for you.'

'Yeah? Just try it.'

'Shut up, or someone'll hear us.'

'They prob'ly know already.'

'Not if you keep your mouth shut.'

'Well I still reckon it's a stupid idea.'

'No one asked you, Clark.'

Pause.

'Well, who else is going off, then? Apart from David?'

'Dave, Pete and me,' said Martin. 'We pretend to get injured, get sent off the field, and Jason, Andrew and Trevor go on.'

'It's not gonna work!'

'But what if our team starts losing the match because Huon and the reserves are playing, huh?'

'We recover from our injuries real quick,' Martin reassured, 'and get ourselves back on the field.'

'Still in it, Trevor? Or have you chickened out?'

'No,' Trevor answered quickly, 'I'm still in.' The anticipation weighed heavily on him. He glanced around at the others and pretended smug self-assurance.

'Better not muck up the game, Huon,' said Bradley Clark, 'or you'll get it from me.'

'You and whose army?' said Martin, who these days seemed to have little time for Bradley's aggression but plenty of time for his own. 'This had better work,' he added, more to himself than to the other kids. Even now, he seemed to be puzzling over the strange piece of generosity he was extending to Trevor.

Gradually, the kids started talking about other things. The game was due to start in fifteen minutes or so, and they nervously checked out their opposition on the other side of the field.

'Could be a hard game.'

'Why?' asked Trevor.

'Last time we played them, they nearly beat us.'

'Look at the size of some of them.'

'Bloody giants!'

'We'll be right. Remember how slack they were in the scrums last time?'

'I still reckon we should forget this dumb plan,' said Bradley.

'Go jump, Clark.'

'Shut up, here's Fuller.'

Fuller immediately checked off the name list in his usual brisk manner. The kids, meanwhile, exchanged guilty, scheming glances and fidgeted around, waiting for the game to commence.

Fuller explained that today was an important match because winning it would virtually secure their chances of making it into the finals '. . . for the third year running,' he added with emphatic hand gestures.

Across the field the teams sized each other up. The parents had arrived armed with the usual dependants and paraphernalia. The clouds above maintained their ominous presence and the air began to chill. The feeling of impatience affecting the team seemed to spread to the parents as well, and they grouped themselves around the team even more closely than usual, alternately offering their respective sons urgent advice and listening to what the coach was saying.

'. . . remember,' said Fuller with the familiar pre-match aggression, 'that team over there are the guys who very nearly beat you a couple of months back. Are they going to beat you today?'

'NO,' came the chorused reply.

'Last week's game was pretty pathetic. Frankly, I was disgusted with this team's general standard of play. This week I want that standard improved. We're going to beat that miserable bunch standing over there and we are going to win this season's competition. Right?'

'RIGHT.'

Fuller moved on to tactics. 'The ground's a bit damp today and a wet ball is a slippery ball, so watch your passes and be ready to dive on any loose ball from them. I want to see you moving up quickly today. Knock them over! I want to see you put them on the ground! Their forwards are big, so I want to see a fair bit of back line play to run their front line around and tire them out. Stretch their defences so that our forwards won't be running into theirs so much. Because they're big, go in with two-man tackles – one over, one under. Break up their defence pattern with little kicks. Give them hell! What are you going to give them?'

'HELL!'

'We've won this comp two years running. You can play badly and lose everything, or you can play your best and win – keep up the proud record. Are you going to win or lose?'

'WIN.'

'Well then,' Fuller said with a satisfied grin, 'who's the best team in the district?'

'CLUB UNDER TWELVES!' the team shouted back, before charging on to the field to the cheers and claps of their audience. Almost simultaneously there was shouting and cheering from the other sideline, and the opposing team also ran on to take their field positions.

Seated on the sideline, Trevor watched with mounting apprehension.

From his prop position on the field, Martin briefly turned around and gave Trevor a thumbs up for good luck. Trevor returned the gesture.

In the middle of the field they were flipping a coin for the kick-off. Seconds later, Bradley Clark was positioning the ball and lining it up for the game's start.

A hush fell over the spectators. The three reserves sat behind the sidelines, beset with secret suspense, and on the field Bradley took his backward paces from the positioned ball. The referee's whistle sounded, the ball was kicked into the air, and the suddenly frenzied parents began their shouted commentary and commands.

'Get them, Scott!'

'Tackle them hard!'

'Rub their noses in the mud!'

'Come on, team!'

'Get them!'

And Fuller as usual, paced up and down the sideline, watching and shouting.

The opposition had the ball, and with some fast running and fast passing, were launching a good offensive. Fuller's team, however, playing with their usual rehearsed precision, were quickly able to bring the opposing players down in a series of fast tackles.

At first, it looked good.

Trevor and the reserves exchanged pensive glances. A short distance behind them stood Kath and Buckley, and Trevor looked at them also, wondering what they were thinking as they watched the football match. Trevor turned away quickly, unnerved by his parents' silence. Today, it seemed that they were more than just cynical onlookers. It was as though they sensed an anticlimax of sorts.

Ten minutes into the game, and so far no score.

Fuller's team had the ball now, and the forwards were moving by degrees from their own end of the field towards the scoring try line. The ground, already soft from the night's drizzle, was slowly becoming more difficult to run on. With an effort, the two teams maintained solidarity and consistently blocked each other's attempts to score points. The tense nil-all atmosphere was beginning to show on

Fuller's face as his sideline commands grew louder and more aggressive.

'Pass that ball out, Under Twelves! Run! What's wrong with you today?'

At last, it happened. David Briggs, running with the ball, was tackled by several kids from the opposing team. Nothing seemed out of the ordinary at first, but David crouched on the muddy ground and didn't get up. The game came to a halt as the referee and then Fuller ran up to where David was. The spectators, suddenly subdued, watched as David was helped limping from the field by Fuller.

'On the field, Evans!' the coach commanded as he sat David down on the reserve bench and started examining the apparently twisted ankle. Mr and Mrs Briggs hovered about in a worried fashion, and David winced convincingly.

The game continued.

Jason Evans had taken on David's field position and was now helping spearhead a new try line attack by the team. Stubbornly, the opposition continued to block the way with fierce tackles. The two teams' aggression was being increased by their growing frustration at their inability to score points.

The parents' shouting continued unabated, a lively noise beneath the imposing sky of grey cloud. On the reserve bench, David Briggs continued to nurse his supposedly injured ankle.

'Well, you're no bloody good for the time being, are you?' barked Fuller, and stalked off to keep an eye on the game.

'Good one, Dave,' whispered Andrew Willis, the other reserve, once there seemed to be no adults within earshot.

'Shut up, you dummy,' David whispered back. 'You'll get us sprung.'

Minutes before the half-time whistle, it happened again.

This time, it was Martin Grace running with the ball. He was just across the halfway line when he collided very convincingly with a kid who seemed to be at least a fraction taller and heavier than Martin. The two of them spun and collapsed to the ground amid a howl of dismay from the crowd.

Once again play was stopped. After the necessary attention from the respective coaches and the referee, the other player hobbled back to his team. Martin however, did not, and Fuller spent a few moments on the field talking to him in a low voice. Martin was hanging painfully on to one shoulder, and somehow, it looked anything but an act.

'Willis!' Fuller shouted, 'get on the field!'

Andrew Willis obligingly stood up and jogged on, as Martin slowly walked off. No sooner had he sat down than he was beseiged by his concerned parents.

'I'm all right, Mum,' he grumbled in reply to his mother's anxious questions.

'Well, I hope so,' Mrs Grace replied seriously. 'It would be a shame if you were to miss out on any more games . . .' She shot Trevor an accusing glance.

Finally the Graces left Martin in peace and resumed their positions nearby in the crowd.

'Does it hurt?' Trevor asked.

Martin came very close to laughing, but didn't. 'Course it does,' he whispered back. 'I'm not pretending. Look at the bruise. I banged me head too, so it's for real.' Then he added, 'You're on next, Trev.'

At half-time Fuller was reduced to shouting about the team's apparent incompetence. 'What's wrong with you lot? Have those other blokes got you scared or something?'

Bradley Clark ventured a reply. 'No sir, but–'

'What do you mean, "No sir, but"?' Fuller sneered. 'I'm finding it hard to believe you're the same team that's won the comp two seasons running. You're like a bunch of girls out on that field today . . .' Taking advantage of the team's ashamed silence, Fuller spoke on loudly about tactics and the lack of them.

'I want to see you doing something out there! We're playing two reserves now, so it's up to the rest of you to win this game. You're not varying your attack; the defence is good but you must do more with the ball. Our wingers have hardly had any possession. Okay, play it in the forwards for a couple of tackles and then use your faster back line . . . I want to see you running hard! Run till you drop! And score points, because if you lose this game today,' Fuller added in an icy voice, 'just forget about winning for the rest of the season.'

The last comment left a dangerous feeling in the air. The team members glanced at each other, thinking perhaps that the plan had gone far enough. Bradley Clark and a few other kids were shooting David Briggs and Martin angry or anxious looks. Resolutely, David and Martin returned the expressions.

By now, the parents had filtered through the team and were offering individual advice in Fuller's temporary absence.

'What's the matter with you today, Michael? I saw you miss three tackles.'

'One dollar for every try, Bradley . . .'

'If I see you drop that ball once again, Scott, no TV for a week!'

'What're you frightened of, Michael? Getting your knees dirty, or something?'

'Just tackle them hard. And stick the knee in on the way down, son.'

'. . . and fifty cents for every field goal, Bradley.'

Fuller returned to this climate of mutual displeasure and resumed his shouted commands on tactics.

115

From a short distance away, Trevor sensed that Peter, the third 'injury', might be about to yield to Fuller's threats and so chicken out. He sat down on the reserve bench with David and Martin as Fuller launched into a last-minute morale booster.

'What are we going to give them?'

'HELL!'

'Are we going to win or lose?'

'WIN!'

'Who's the best team in the district?'

'CLUB UNDER TWELVES!'

'Maybe you should go back on,' Trevor whispered to Martin.

'No,' Martin replied. 'If we lose it'll be Fuller's fault, not mine.'

Seconds later, the teams were reassembled on the field. The opposition kicked the ball off, and like mechanical toys Fuller's team came to life.

And then the inevitable happened.

The grey clouds finally yielded a fine mist of rain across the town. There was a chorused groan from the spectators as the mist increased to a drizzle. Overcoats and umbrellas slowly appeared as a coloured canopy against the shower, while on the field the football game continued relentlessly. And just as it looked as though the final part of Martin's plan had been abandoned, it was unintentionally completed.

The opposition had the ball and were moving across the wet field. Fuller's team ran up and closed in as the opposing team methodically passed the ball out along their line of players until the kid at the end was left to make the short dash for the try line. Bradley Clark, however, was not far behind, and with a desperate burst of energy, lunged at the player and tried to tackle him.

But somewhere on the way down, Bradley's foot slipped on the wet ground and he fell heavily on to one knee. His left hand had just grasped the opposing player's ankle, enough to make the boy stumble and lose his grip on the ball. In the confusion of movement the wayward ball was knocked on and the referee's whistle sounded.

Everyone started to organize themselves into a scrum except for Bradley, who was having trouble standing up.

'This is bloody incredible,' Martin said in a low voice. 'Clark's really hurt himself.'

'How d' you know?' Trevor asked.

'Well look at his face. He's nearly bawling.' Martin suppressed a smile. 'Tough toenails for Clark. Serves him right for trying to be such a smarty.'

'What happens now, though?'

'Dunno. We've never had this many real injuries in one match before.'

They briefly watched the on-field drama as the referee and Fuller confirmed that Brad's knee was definitely out of action for the time being. There were concerned noises from the parents on the sidelines.

The rain continued to drizzle down and another lull of silence swept over the crowd as Fuller quickly decided what to do next. He swiftly turned to the reserve bench.

'Briggs!' he shouted. 'Can you run on that ankle yet?'

It was David Briggs's parents who answered for him. 'He's not going on that field injured,' they said, with a surprising note of rebellion.

'Grace!' the coach shouted then, 'what about you?'

Martin silently displayed his shoulder, which by now was vividly bruised and beyond vigorous use. Fuller gritted his teeth in exasperation and turned quickly to the field. 'Jason Evans, you're playing Clark's forward position ...' And then he realized the next problem. 'Are you two sure you can't play?' he asked Martin and David.

Their reply was silent and negative.

Valuable time was being lost. Fuller moved up to where Trevor was sitting at the end of the reserve bench. With some difficulty, Trevor looked up and saw the man's rain-wet, intimidating face.

'I don't trust you, Huon. You're a liar and a sneak ...'

At that moment, Buckley moved up beside Trevor, a defensively angry look on his face.

Aware of this, Fuller continued in a low voice, 'Get on that field and play, Huon. You're five eighth, and you'd better play well, boy. I'll be watching.' The coach stalked off.

Trevor sprang up and ran on to the field. The other kids looked at him blankly, almost disbelievingly, as he appeared amongst them and lined himself up adjacent to the re-formed scrum. Brushing the wet hair from his forehead, he pulled the headband from his shorts' pocket and put it on. For one short moment his eyes found his parents, who were sheltering from the rain under one of Buckley's coats. Quickly he tried to read their expressions – encouraging, concerned, anticipating – and then realized that now he was on his own.

Fleetingly, he could also see Fuller's angry face. Bringing his attention back to what was happening around him, he joined the team as they fought their way back across the halfway line, trying desperately to anticipate their movements, to apply what he'd spent an eternity watching from the sidelines.

The drizzle of rain intensified again as the referee's whistle blew, and the scrum commenced their wrestling for the ball's possession. Seconds later the ball was sent skating from the ruck into Michael O'Leary's hands. He turned quickly and sent the ball into Trevor's anxious grasp. Breaking into an erratic half-run, Trevor swung sideways and passed the ball on to Jason Evans and the front row.

There had been no time to think. Everything had just happened, and miraculously, had happened the right way.

Grimly, the game continued.

So did the rain, in steady opposition. It soaked both teams alike until their hair and football clothes clung to them, cold and uncomfortable. Every time one of them was tackled he came up caked with mud and grime, because the grass cover was gradually losing out to the wet and the pounding of football boots. But still the spectators' shouting and enthusiasm urged them on against the elements.

Carefully, Trevor kept an eye on the opposition. At close range, they were as large and fast as had been feared, and played with a speed and aggression that Fuller's team seemed to find it hard to cope with, let alone overcome. Suddenly someone shouted, 'Trevor!'

He turned to see the ball sailing in his direction. Miraculously he caught it and attempted to run ahead, but found his path blocked by members of the opposing team. Quickly he sidetracked, found Michael O'Leary running parallel to him, and clumsily passed the ball out. Just as quickly, Michael was tackled. He stumbled up, and the ball was passed out again. Suddenly caught in the very midst of play, Trevor found the ball in his hands once more. His mind spun dizzily, and he ran.

Jason Evans yelled, 'Kick it!'

Just short of being tackled, Trevor managed to give the ball a running punt. It sailed through the air, missing everything except for the waiting hands of the opposition. Now the tables were neatly turned, as Fuller's team headed across the field in hot pursuit of the opposition.

They were either too slow or too late, or maybe the field was just too muddy in the wrong places. At any rate, an opposing player made a last marathon dash, beating the efforts of pursuers to cross the try line and triumphantly thump the ball down on the ground. There was wild cheering from the opposition's parents, and an almost stunned silence from Fuller's side of the field.

And then, in final insult, the shower of rain turned to a downpour.

As far as the referee was concerned, this was the last straw, and he blew his whistle, frantically indicating for everyone to leave the field. At this command, kids and parents alike scattered in all directions to shelter. Trevor, not seeing Kath and Buckley anywhere in sight, ran quickly back to where the Kombi was parked.

Kath and Buckley sat inside, wet and dishevelled, and Trevor hastily scrambled in beside them.

'Welcome aboard the Titanic,' said Kath with a grin.

The interior of the Kombi was deathly cold and the insides of the windows had begun to fog up. From the vantage point of the front seat, they watched the last of the drenched spectators dash across to a parked car.

Buckley was laughing. 'That would have to be the funniest spectacle I've witnessed for some time. All those manic parents. All those poor kids . . .' He looked at Trevor. 'So you finally got to play, huh?'

Trevor sighed very loudly. 'Yes.'

'And what was it like?'

'All right,' Trevor answered, because he felt neither satisfaction nor disappointment. Just fatigue, and cold.

They sat in the Kombi for five, ten minutes. The rain thudded heavily on the van roof, and all over the town and surrounding valley could be seen the hazy sweep of the storm.

After a while, carloads of people began to leave, and Buckley said slowly, 'I think that's the end of it.'

And just as abruptly as he had been thrown into the day's confusion, so Trevor left it. Barely twenty minutes ago it had finished and yet already it felt oddly distant. On the field there had been little time to think, but now as they drove home through the rain to the caravan park, time stretched forever.

He was momentarily aware of a faint, almost intangible distance from his parents and all that he knew. The day had been a measure of his own independence, but a price had been paid for it. Uncomfortably, he was reminded of the deceit and realized how intensely he disliked trying to be what he wasn't.

Much later, he sat at the table in the caravan, carefully and laboriously finishing off the story for Mr Fuller. It had become a story about lots of things. There was himself, Buckley and Kath, and a life story compressed into twelve pages of an exercise book. In weary defiance he thought to himself, *I don't care what Fuller says about what I've written.*

Something was not quite right, and for a moment he no longer felt like Trevor Huon, but like a faceless stranger.

He lay awake that night on the bunk in the Kombi, reliving the day and the four weeks beforehand. In the caravan, Kath and Buckley weren't playing familiar songs on their guitars; they were talking. Their voices rose and fell, and it was difficult to hear or understand what they were saying. They almost seemed to be arguing, but Trevor reassured himself that this was an impossibility, since Kath and Buckley never seemed to argue.

For a while, he could have been asleep. When he next opened his eyes, the van door was open, throwing light from the caravan around the inside of the Kombi. Buckley was sitting at the end of the bunk.

'Hullo,' he said softly.

Trevor sat up and rested one elbow on his pillow.

'I've come to talk to you,' Buckley added.

'What about?'

'About . . . lots of things.'

Trevor said nothing.

'Right, now Trev, you and I have got to be very honest with each other.'

'Why?'

'Because sometimes your mum and I worry about you. Now is one of those times. Watching the football today, watching all those crazy people. It really was pretty weird . . . Trevor, what do you really think of the life we lead?'

'What d' you mean?'

'Moving around all the time. Doing seasonal work and odd jobs. Staying in caravan parks.'

'I like it,' Trevor said with resolve.

'Really?'

'Yes, really.'

'Kath and I thought a long time ago what a good thing it'd be for a child of ours to have the experience. To go places, explore the country, meet different people and see how they live. Let you know there are more than one set of rules for living. It *sounds* great, but it's also a bit lonely, isn't it?'

'Yeah. Sometimes.'

There was an awkward silence. Buckley looked away for a moment, stroking his beard thoughtfully.

'Sometimes though,' Trevor said after some thought, 'I really wish we could stop travelling and stay in one place to live.'

Buckley grimaced. 'But imagine living in a town like this all the time, Trev. To be accepted by anyone, you'd have to be like them. I wouldn't like to imagine you becoming like the kids here, but I think that's already started to happen.'

'No, it hasn't!' Trevor replied indignantly. 'I got into the football team to prove I wasn't as bad as they reckoned. I wanted them to like me, I didn't want to *be* like them.'

In agreement, Buckley nodded. 'I understand.'

'I wouldn't want to stay in a place like this, anyway,' said Trevor.

'Where, then?' promoted Buckley.

The answer was an obvious one that pictured itself clearly in Trevor's mind. *The house*, he thought, but knew how weak and far fetched it might sound in the daylight of Buckley's commonsense.

'I don't know,' he said finally.

For a moment, the two of them gazed seriously at each other, trying to extract some mutual understanding.

'We're going to be leaving,' Buckley said then. 'Staying here and putting up with what you have been serves no point. When would you like to leave?'

Trevor brightened. 'Next week?' he suggested.

'Next week it is,' Buckley replied quietly.

Kath stepped into the Kombi then, leant over and silently kissed Trevor goodnight, and sat on the bunk next to Buckley.

There were still things Trevor wanted to say, but was not quite sure how they should be said. Slowly he lay down again, cocooned himself within the sleeping bag and the blankets, and stared mutely into the semi-darkness.

For another stretch of unknown time, he could have been asleep again. When he opened his eyes once more, it was still dark. And his parents were still sitting at the end of the bunk, looking back at him almost sadly.

Thirteen

Buckley picked up a familiar looking exercise book and placed it on the dining table next to Trevor.

'Found this here last night after you and I had our talk. We read your story.'

'Oh,' Trevor replied hesitantly. *So now they know.* It didn't seem to matter so much this morning. He looked down again, seemingly engrossed in the bowl of muesli before him, trying to imagine the circumstances that would shortly meet him at school. *Today is Monday*, he thought to himself yet again. *Yesterday was Sunday. Today is the day after the game.*

'Sorry,' Buckley started to apologize. 'Hope you didn't mind us reading it.'

'No,' Trevor said, not sure whether he minded or not.

Kath walked into the leaden silence that seemed to occupy the caravan. Seriously, she watched as Trevor quietly ate breakfast and as Buckley clutched the exercise book, trying to think of the next thing to say.

'We read it several times,' she said, and switched on the electric jug. 'It was really good, Trevor.' He looked up at her, and she added, 'I mean that.'

'Yeah,' he said slowly. *Today is Monday*. 'I'm going to get into trouble, but.'

'Why?' Buckley asked.

'Because Mr Fuller wanted me to write something imaginary and I wrote about something real. The first time I

124

wrote it, he made me do it again and told me to write something different, or else.'

Buckley sighed, 'Are you pleased with your story?'

Trevor nodded. 'I think it's the best thing I've ever done at school.'

His parents nodded in some sort of agreement. Kath sat down next to Buckley and Trevor, mouth full of cereal, looked over at them, waiting for something more to be said.

'Did you really mean everything you wrote?' Kath asked.

'What d' you mean?'

'About living in a caravan. About moving.'

'Yes I did.'

At a loss for words again, they fell silent, exchanging self-conscious looks in an attempt to convey their thoughts. Trevor took note of the pensive expressions on his parents' faces before allowing himself to become once more besieged by the threat of the approaching day at school, by the certain aftermath of the weekend's football match. The successful image of Mr Fuller's football team lay in pieces around him, and he was feeling at least partly responsible for the Sunday afternoon that had run out of control. *What happens now*? he mused.

Buckley spoke up. 'What you said last night ...'

'About what?' Trevor asked.

'About moving,' his father reminded him.

'Oh,' he answered thoughtfully. 'Yes.'

'Do you still want to leave next week?'

'Yes,' he said quickly.

Buckley nodded. 'I'm finishing up work on Wednesday. We can get on the road first thing Thursday morning, which is this week.' Inquiringly, he looked at Trevor for a response, but none was forthcoming. 'I've had enough of bricklaying,' he added with a reassuring smile, 'enough of this town. I think we all need a change.'

125

'Where will we go?' Trevor asked.

'Haven't decided yet,' Kath answered. 'But probably somewhere we've been before.'

Something in her reply intrigued Trevor, and it seemed to him that she and Buckley had already decided on a destination. *Where*? he wondered, but did not ask them aloud. He smiled and settled back in his seat, considering the week's new perspective.

'We're leaving Thursday morning?' he asked again, just to make sure. 'This week?'

'Yep. Is that all right?'

He nodded. 'It's all right. It's terrific.' Three more days of school.

At last Buckley stood up. 'I must be going. Be late for work, otherwise.'

Kath looked at her watch. 'You'll be late for school, too,' she told Trevor. 'I'll write you a note to take.'

Buckley was at the caravan doorway. 'You know all those things in your story?' he said. 'What you wrote about the beach, and the house where we used to live?' He paused. 'Do you think about it that much?'

Trevor stared back at his father, wanting to be still in bed, with the sheets and blankets hiding his face and all that he felt. 'Yes, I guess I do,' he answered with an effort.

Buckley turned to leave, then stopped and said, 'You know what? So do I.'

Trevor thought about that for a while.

Kath wrote out a brief note of excuse for Mr Fuller and then drove Trevor to school in the Kombi.

'Got your story with you?' she asked as he clambered out at the school gate.

He nodded. 'Yeah, it's in m' bag. See you, Mum.'

'See you later.'

The school was shrouded in its usual Monday morning quiet. He could hear good morning songs being sung in the kindergarten classroom, spelling lists being chanted in one of the primary grade rooms. Quickly, he crossed the empty stretch of asphalt playground, thankful for having missed the ritual of morning assembly, and yet feeling strange to be beginning the day differently. At the steps of his own classroom he hesitated before climbing the steps to the doorway.

From their rows of desks, the class paused to regard his presence. And from his usual position beside the blackboard, Mr Fuller looked at Trevor coldly before ordering the class back to their maths work.

'Come in!' he commanded, in a half-shout.

Trevor quietly walked in, struggling to control his nervousness.

'Have you,' the teacher demanded aggressively, 'any sort of civilized excuse for this lateness?'

Trevor nodded, rummaged around in the shoulderbag and pulled out Kath's handwritten note. Mr Fuller took the note and impatiently waved Trevor to his seat. Once at his desk, Trevor got out his maths book and wrote a few intent lines of sums, aware of the furtive glances being directed at him from the occupants of the surrounding desks. He and Martin exchanged rudimentary good morning expressions, and Martin surreptitiously pushed a piece of paper across the desk for Trevor's inspection. On it was a blue biro drawing of a skull and cross-bones, plus a helpful scrawled comment that read, 'You're in the pooh today, mate.'

Mr Fuller, meanwhile, was embarking on another exercise in classroom embarrassment. For the benefit of the class, he held up Trevor's excuse note and read aloud what Kath had written.

Dear Mr Fuller,

Please excuse Trevor's slight lateness this morning, as he slept in some forty-five minutes. This was probably due to the exhilarating game of football played yesterday afternoon, a physically and intellectually taxing affair at the best of times. As a coach and teacher, I'm sure you're well aware of such things.

> Yours faithfully,
> Katherine Huon.

Trevor kept his head lowered, trying to concentrate on the maths. For a moment, he felt nothing but mild hostility as the other kids giggled appreciatively. But his mother's offbeat sense of humour suddenly dawned on him, and he grinned.

Mr Fuller caught his smirk. 'I'm not amused,' the teacher retorted angrily, screwing the note up. 'And you, Huon, are one of several people I intend talking to at tomorrow afternoon's training. Until then, I have no desire to talk about football, or the weekend's game. Consider yourself in trouble, son. You and fifteen other members of this class.'

An orderly hush once more filled the room, as everyone huddled dutifully over exercise books. Trevor and Martin exchanged glances again, Martin as much as to say, 'I told you so.'

Trevor sighed inaudibly, hoping that the worst had passed. He was wrong.

Not five minutes later, Mr Fuller's voice boomed out. 'Your written expression book. Huon!'

Trevor looked up.

'Your written expression book,' the teacher repeated. 'You've got it with you, of course?'

'Yes.'

'Sir!'

'Yes sir,' Trevor replied, pulling the book from shoulder-bag and holding it up.

'I'm not your servant, son. Bring it here!'

Face set, Trevor walked rigidly to the teacher's desk and handed the book over.

'You've finished your *new* story?' Mr Fuller flicked through the book, ignoring Trevor's anxious nod. 'How long is your story, Huon?'

'Twelve pages. Sir.'

'Then perhaps,' Mr Fuller said slowly, 'you'd like to read it to us.'

Trevor looked back, expressionless, until the request registered. He shook his head.

The teacher's attention was elsewhere. 'Pens down, everybody,' he said to the class. 'We are about to hear Trevor Huon's story.' There was an obedient clatter of biros being placed on desks as the class turned its collective but bewildered attention to Trevor, who was still shaking his head.

'What's the matter?' the teacher asked with mock concern.

'I don't want to read it. Sir.'

'You'll do as you're told! Now read us your story. We're all waiting.' Ready to enjoy the whole procedure, the teacher sat back in his chair, arms folded. The class watched with a mixture of anticipation and controlled pity, because most of them knew what it was Trevor had written in the book he now unwillingly held.

Slowly he opened the book at the first page, stared blankly at his words and sentences.

'We're waiting, Huon,' said Mr Fuller evenly.

Trevor felt giddy, sick, angry.

'Once . . .' he started with an effort.

'Louder!'

He stood on the vacant stretch of floorboards between the blackboard and the rows of desks, the deathly silence all around him. His mind wrestled with a dozen different urges and feelings for a moment more, and then dully, he began to read.

'Once, there was a beach. That's the place I remember best, and I often seem to dream about it when I'm asleep in the Kombi, and we're moving . . .'

He read the first few sentences nervously. When he looked up at the other kids, he saw with surprise that their faces were neither judging nor critical. With mute intensity they waited for him to continue, and resisting the urge to check Mr Fuller's expression, Trevor went on.

'The house we lived in was old and rambling . . .'

He read about himself, a little child of three or four – skin tanned, hair as white as the sand where he stood. Waves lapped lazily at his feet and he could feel the heat of the sun on his back. The beach – it stretched as far as he could see. And home was a maze of dim, cool rooms, a clutter of wooden furniture and a jungle of pot plants.

'And one day, this all changed. We bought the caravan, and left the house behind. Suddenly, there was the moving from town to town, the living in caravan parks and beside orchards . . .' He read about the inconvenience and the travel, the journeying across far-flung countryside. He read about the pear picking at Tatura, the orange orchards at Boundary Bend, places called Bathurst, Griffith and Young.

'. . . because sometimes, it's not an easy life. It's hard to make friends or stay friends with someone for long, because you go to maybe six different schools a year. Sometimes, people look down on us, call us gypsies and no-hopers, which is knocking what they don't understand.

130

Teachers often think the children of fruitpickers are all stupid, and treat us that way. For some kids that's true, because it's often hard to learn much, but it can also be unfair . . .'

The words were getting hard to read again. In his own terms, they were about being the outsider and being alone. They were about the present time, but also about the past and all the friendships that had lasted for six or eight weeks of a year, but no longer. They were about the notion of wanting to belong somewhere. But permeating his carefully written sentences was hope too, the optimism he'd inherited from Kath and Buckley.

With relief, he came to the last page.

'. . . all the time spent moving has had its bad points, but there are good things too. I have met lots of people, young and old, and have probably learnt a lot from them. I have seen more of Australia than most kids my age – the cities and the country towns, the arid plains of the outback, the green hills of the coast, and the thousands of miles of roads and highways that have taken me to these places.'

He paused.

'But sometimes, I still think about the beach and the old house I was born in. That's my real home. Someday I'll go back there.'

Slowly he closed the book.

'That's the end,' he said softly, looking down.

At first, no one said anything. The other kids returned his expressionless gaze, as if they expected more of the story to follow. Mr Fuller maintained the uncharacteristic silence that had left the story oddly uninterrupted. Tentatively, Trevor held the exercise book out for him to take.

'I don't want it,' the teacher said suddenly. 'Sit down where you belong, and take your book with you.'

Trevor walked back to his seat, placed the exercise book

carefully back in the shoulderbag, and sat down. As he did so, he distantly heard Mr Fuller's voice. 'Right. Who has not yet finished the maths work on the blackboard . . .?'

The football match post-mortem came later.

Mid-morning break had the kids grouped in the playground, voices raised in debate and disagreement.

'It was your fault, O'Leary. Kept hogging the ball.'

'Yeah. If you'd passed it out instead of –'

'Aw come on! There I was up near the try line with a bunch of the opposition coming towards me. Where were you lot; halfway up the other bloody end!'

'Were not!'

'Were so.'

'Every time we had the ball we lost it because no one was up there with it.'

'How about the opposition, but? Twice the size of us, prob'ly twice the weight.'

'Twice as fast, too.'

'And you and your stupid ideas, Grace,' Brad Clark said to Martin with contempt, 'getting half the team off the field just so bloody Huon could get on.'

'Shut up, or Fuller'll find out.'

'He'll find out, anyway. We'll all get into trouble, then. Huon was no good, like I said.'

'Rack off, Brad. He was okay. Weren't you, Trev?'

Trevor shrugged.

'He was okay for a beginner.'

'Okay for a little guy,' added Scott McKay generously.

'Fat lot of good it did, anyway,' Bradley continued mockingly. 'He got the ball twice, which proves he can't play, and never could. Bull artist, Huon. Now *we* get into trouble off Fuller.'

'First game we lost in two seasons.'

'You'll never get to play again, Huon,' Bradley added.
'Give up now, while you can.'

'Fuller won't do anything,' Martin said.

'Why not?'

'What about this morning? He told Trev last week to
write a different story or else, and what happens? Fuller
doesn't do anything. And he won't.'

'How d'you know?'

'Trev's got it all over Fuller.'

'Only because he's weak –'

'Rack off, Brad. Never seen you stand up to Fuller.'

'Aw crap . . .' Bradley responded, but for the time being
said no more.

'How come he didn't do anything, Trevor?'

'Don't know,' Trevor said, puzzled. 'I really thought he
would.'

'He didn't even say anything.'

'Prob'ly thinking up a punishment for you.'

'One million lines: "I must do as I'm told".'

'Two months picking up papers in the playground.'

'Letter home to your parents.'

'Yeah, you know – get your mum and dad up to school
for an interview.'

'They'd stick up for me, anyway,' Trevor said.

'Your story was good.'

'Yeah, better than mine.'

'Was most of it true?'

'All of it was,' Trevor replied, not really wanting to talk
about it.

'That's what it's really like in a caravan?'

'Did you really write it?'

'Course I did.'

'Huh! Your parents probably helped you.'

'I did it by myself.'

133

'Bull. Bet your parents helped you write it.'

'I did it by myself,' Trevor repeated.

'It was pretty good, anyway.'

'You're better at writing than you are at footy.'

'Bet you're the one Fuller's gonna blow up at training tomorrow, Trevor.'

'Reckon. He'll prob'ly tell you to leave the team.'

'Worse than that. You haven't seen him really mad, yet.'

'He goes off his brain!'

'You coming to training tomorrow?'

Trevor shook his head.

'Yeah,' Bradley said mockingly, 'you're just a chicken, Huon.'

'How come you're not coming to training?'

Trevor looked distantly at the assembled group, feeling almost as though he had already left.

'Because,' he answered, 'I'm leaving on Thursday.'

Fourteen

The very last morning, he felt a strange sort of immunity.

Eyes closed and half-dreaming, he marvelled at the strength, of sorts, that he'd found in himself. All of a sudden this had happened, in a few weeks, in the time it had taken to live in this town. Over and over again, he pictured himself standing in the classroom, reading his story – left-handed scribble in an exercise book. The words and phrases came back to him now, mingled with all the other thoughts, memories and descriptions he hadn't had the time or patience to write.

And Fuller didn't like it, he marvelled. *The best thing that I've ever done. But he listened all the same.* Here Trevor paused, because the teacher's attitude was still beyond understanding.

Why did he listen?

When Trevor eventually opened his eyes, it was to squint grumpily around the familiar interior of the Kombivan. Grumpily, because he hadn't had enough sleep. Squinting, because the sunlight seemed to have found his tired face through the window. The blankets barely covered him now and lay in heaped disarray at the bottom of the bunk. That left only the sleeping bag between him and the chilly early morning. As usual, it was hopelessly twisted around so that the zipper was somewhere underneath him instead of being on top and down the front where he could reach it.

Anyway, it was a good excuse to remain horizontal and

135

so for another half hour or so, he did, until Kath's voice called him from the caravan.

'You'll be late for school, Trevor.'

Today is Wednesday.

Things were coming to an end. Buckley dressed in his bricklaying clothes and left early for his last day at the club. The caravan that morning rang with the sound of his enthusiastic voice, his obvious happiness at the approaching change of scenery.

'You haven't changed your mind?' he asked Trevor yet again.

'No,' Trevor answered with resolve, 'I haven't changed my mind.' His mind in fact was already working overtime, trying to unravel the mystery of where they might be going to next. Several times he had asked Kath and Buckley, but the answer remained the same.

'We still haven't decided.'

By the afternoon, Kath would have the tent annexe dismantled and stored away. Everything would be packed once more, the caravan would be hitched to the Kombi, and tomorrow at dawn they would set off.

Kath was writing another note to Mr Fuller.

'Writing anything funny, Mum?'

'No, not this time. Just telling him you're leaving.'

He stepped outside into the reluctant August sunshine, hitched the patchwork shoulderbag over one arm, and set off. A short distance from the Kombi and caravan, however, he stopped, turned and headed back. Inside the Kombi, he rummaged through the cupboards under his bunk.

'Forget something?' Kath called from the caravan.

He stepped out of the Kombi. 'Yeah. This,' he replied, and held up the soccer ball.

The town's morning stillness gradually diminished as the

sunlight took its hold. Sporadic traffic littered the orderly streets, the last of the dawn's patchy mists cleared from the treetops, and as a familiar background noise came the hum and clatter of the timber mill at work.

Trevor walked the length of the sprawling main street, taking in for the last time the faded rural shopfronts, his own shuffling reflection in the plate glass, the cold stateliness of the war memorial. He kicked over the debris from the towering Norfolk pines, leaving his footprints as dust-bare patches in the carpet of fallen brown needles. And as he came closer and closer to the school, the ambling procession of children increased around him, a noisy, energetic array of grey school uniforms.

'Look, you guys!'

'Hey, check Huon out!'

'He's brought his soccer ball.'

'Taking up your wog's game again, huh?'

He passed the kids in the playground, walked on to the classroom and entered, putting Kath's note in a prominent position on Mr Fuller's desk. He left the soccer ball in relative safety on the floor beside his own desk.

Outside in the playground once more, he strolled over to the fringes of the group of boys, who by now had found something else to talk and argue about.

Martin Grace gave Trevor a quick nudge.

'How come you brought your soccer ball?'

Trevor made a face. 'I don't know,' he said, still mildly wondering about it himself. 'I just did.'

Martin shook his head in disbelief. 'Jeez you're mad. You really are.'

'I know,' Trev replied with a half grin.

'What're you going to do with it, then?' Martin demanded critically. 'Play soccer by yourself all day?'

'Might as well,' Trevor said.

'Nut case, Huon,' Martin said, rolling his eyes. 'Nut case.'

'What happened at training?'

'Yesterday?'

'Yeah.'

'Huh. Heaps.'

'What was it like?'

'Like . . .' Martin paused for a comparison, 'like the time Fuller sprung you. First, he ran us into the ground and then he told us off. You know, two hundred laps of the oval, one thousand push-ups and touch-toes, jogging on the spot till our legs dropped off –'

'Aw, come on. What happened then?'

'Then he threw his usual mental, telling us what pansies we were, and all that. Just for losing a game. Reckons the premiership's as good as lost, now. He just doesn't want to admit the other team were better than us.'

'Did he say anything about me?'

Martin laughed. 'Did he what! As much as blamed you for everything, and doesn't want you on the team any more. Does he know you're leaving?'

'Left a note from my mum on his desk, so he'll know soon.'

'You should join a footy team where you're going next. If you practised, you'd be an all right player.'

Trevor shook his head. 'I'd rather play for fun.'

'I reckon you're mad. Still leaving tomorrow?'

Trevor nodded.

In the clockwork precision of the classroom, the kids wrote out maths exercises, grammar exercises, completed reading work. Mr Fuller hovered ominously between his desk and the blackboard, ever watchful for those not working attentively enough.

At his desk beside Martin, Trevor worked quietly, but with no particular neatness or care. Concerned only with the day's gradually approaching conclusion, he found himself somehow escaping the attention of the teacher. In fact, he suddenly realized Mr Fuller had said virtually nothing to him since Monday, the morning he had read the story. When Trevor looked up once or twice from his schoolwork, he found the teacher looking critically back at him, and knew instinctively that the note from Kath had been read.

Nothing more was said about the story, either. When Mr Fuller paced the aisles of desks handing everyone else back their written expression books, Trevor remembered that his hadn't been given to the teacher. Instead, he had taken it home and put it away in a cupboard in the Kombi. He supposed that Mr Fuller didn't want to know anything more about it.

Beside him, Martin flicked his book open.

'A "C",' he whispered indignantly. 'The ratbag only gave me a "C" for my story. Just because he doesn't like science fiction ...'

At lunchtime, Trevor walked slowly outside with the soccer ball, despite Martin's disconcerted remarks of, 'You're not going to play with that, are you?'

'Course I am. Think I was going to eat it, or something?'

'No, but ...'

Trevor walked off, bouncing the soccer ball. A short distance away in the other direction stood the rest of the kids, and it was towards this group that Martin reluctantly gravitated.

'Hey, Huon!' shouted Bradley Clark. 'Show us how you play wogball.'

'Let's see how good you are.'

Trevor looked at them vacantly. He felt like a bit of an idiot for having brought the soccer ball at all. Then suddenly, *Stuff them*! he thought. He dropped the ball to the ground and gave it an idle kick. It skated across the playground and he followed after it and kicked it again. Behind him, the kids cheered sarcastically. Trevor kicked the ball again, harder.

The cheering behind him became a confusion of shouts and he heard the pounding of running feet approaching him.

'The ball –'

'Get the ball –'

'Grab it –'

They ran past him in a jostling, shouting herd, and the soccer ball disappeared from his sight.

'Here, Jason.'

'Pass it here.'

'Out to me –'

'No, me.'

'Oh no!' Trev said aloud, picturing the soccer ball either being stolen or pitched on to a classroom roof. 'They're going to wreck it.'

Suddenly Martin was next to him. 'No they won't.'

'Why won't they?' Trevor demanded angrily.

'Because,' answered Martin, 'I'll punch their heads in if they do.' He laughed, then grabbed Trevor's shoulder and forced him into a run. 'C'mon, Huon, what're you waiting for?'

They caught up with the running huddle of kids. Somewhere in their midst was the thud of the soccer ball being caught between kicking feet.

'Teams!'

'Teams?'

'We need teams.'

'I'm one captain.'

'Up yours, Clark, I'm captain.'

'Rack off!'

'I'm on Huon's side!' Martin yelled helpfully.

'So 'm I.'

'Me too.'

'Who's on my side then?' demanded Bradley Clark.

'Me!'

'Me!'

'I'm on Huon's side!'

'Rack off, we've got enough. Get on Clark's side and hurry up.'

That was about as far as the organization extended. In two rough teams, they carried out the game across the expanse of the playground, competing with younger kids' games of football and skipping. The sense of fun about the whole thing was infectious, unbelievable. They broke every possible rule, picking the soccer ball up, passing it around, dropping it to the ground once more and kicking it furiously about. Everyone forgot who was on whose team, but after a while it didn't seem to matter anyway. They were still playing a loud, abusive game when the end-of-lunchtime bell rang.

Slowly they ground to a halt, swearing amongst themselves about the shortness of lunchbreaks, before heading back towards Mr Fuller's classroom. Trevor picked up the soccer ball and followed the group across the playground. He could hardly believe what had just happened, and he certainly couldn't understand it. His head pounded and his ankles hurt from where other people's kicks had missed the ball, but somehow it seemed oddly worth it.

He sat through the endlessness of the afternoon, looking blankly at the social studies work he was supposed to be doing and trying not to look at the clock on the wall.

'Great game, huh?' Martin whispered.

'Yeah,' Trevor replied, and grinned politely, mystified by

141

these kids, by this school, by the enveloping town. Absently, he filled the back of his social studies stencil with biro drawings of motorcycles and racing cars. The clock on the wall ticked on, and Trevor daydreamed for an eternity.

'Hey!' Martin's voice suddenly registered. 'Wake up, dummy. Packing up time.'

Around him, the classroom shuffled into life as desks were tidied, papers picked up and books collected.

From the doorway, Mr Fuller issued commands. 'No papers to be left on the floor. Don't forget tonight's homework. Those who do will find themselves with extra work to do.'

Groans.

'It's also,' the teacher added, 'our turn to present an item at next week's school assembly. I want you to think about a song we could sing . . .'

More groans.

'. . . and not some moronic pop song, thank you. Something intelligent.'

Trevor sat emptying the contents of his desk. The collection of stencils he folded and put into the shoulderbag, before methodically going through all the miscellaneous scraps of paper he seemed to have accumulated.

'How long have you been here?' Martin asked.

'Um, about five weeks,' answered Trevor, coming to a carefully folded piece of paper that had his name written on it in multicoloured texta, surrounded by a mass of pink hearts. Puzzled at its mysterious appearance, he opened it long enough to realize that it was from Angela Simmons.

'Five weeks?' Martin replied slowly. 'It seems longer than that.' He suddenly spied the note Trevor was holding. 'Oooh aaah!' he said jubilantly, and snatched it from Trevor's grasp. 'A girlfriend, eh? Who is she?'

'Give it here!' Trevor protested, and proceeded to wrestle

142

it from Martin. After some moments he succeeded, and managed to stuff it safely into the shoulderbag.

Martin giggled, but was suddenly silenced by the intent gaze of Mr Fuller.

'We're waiting for you,' the teacher rebuked, as the remainder of the class assumed orderly positions beside their desks.

Martin stood up as Trevor quickly sorted through the remaining contents of his desk.

'Good afternoon, class,' said Mr Fuller.

'Good afternoon, sir,' they answered in unison, before filing out of the room. Trevor followed on, dumping the scrap papers in the rubbish bin beside the door as he left. He glanced at the teacher, hoping perhaps to see something human about the stern face that briefly met his own. Nothing of course was forthcoming, and Trevor ran a few paces outside to catch up with Martin.

'Bet I know who your girlfriend is,' said Martin. 'Angela.'

Trevor grinned.

Oddly enough, Martin changed the subject. 'You'll be glad to see the last of Fuller, huh?' he said.

'I reckon,' Trevor agreed.

'He didn't even talk to you today. Or yesterday. Wasn't really fair to you; ever since you first came, he gave you a hard time.'

Trevor shrugged. 'I guess he did.'

Martin, not really understanding Trevor's apparently blasé response, made a face. 'You're an idiot. I wouldn't have put up with it.'

They came to the school gate and stopped before heading in their different directions.

'Well, see you, I guess.'

'Yeah. See you.'

'Will you write?' Martin asked then.

'Write? What d' you mean?'

'You know . . . write me a letter. When you get to wherever you're going to. So I know where you are and all that.'

'Oh,' Trevor said, puzzling briefly over the complexities of people who abused you one minute and made requests of you the next. 'Sure,' he replied, seeing the expectant look on Martin's face, 'I'll write.'

'Okay. See you.'

'Yeah. See you.'

There seemed nothing more to say.

Tomorrow

They were in a different place now.

He took a long time to wake up that morning, his closed eyes fighting the glare of the sunlight that shone in through the windows of the Kombi. He squirmed restlessly, trying to fall asleep again.

It seemed such an eternity later, but it was only the following day. Where were they yesterday? In a caravan park in a town far away. In a foreign country, in a time past. Thinking about it like that kept him awake.

All around seemed silent and still. The Kombi was stopped and parked beneath trees. With a start, Trevor sat up, wriggling free of the sleeping bag.

They were parked in bushland, scrub, isolation. At first, there seemed to be no other sound, no clue of civilization. Twisted gum-trees, bushy wattles and sandy grey soil were all he could see through the window next to him. He rolled over, peered out the back window, and was greeted by the same sight of motionless bushland. When he looked a bit harder, he could see early morning dew clinging to strands of grass and to lofty spiderwebs spun between trees.

Where are we? he thought suddenly, and tossed aside blankets and sleeping bag. His curiosity forced him outside, hastily dressed and wondering. Everywhere the sun seemed to be shining, refreshing and unexpectedly warm. Of Buckley and Kath there was no sign and for a moment he stood puzzled beside the Kombi.

It was only then that he became aware of a noise some-where nearby – a hissing, roaring background to the silence of the surrounding bushland. The noise grew louder, faded, grew louder once more.

His sleepy mind struggled to awaken and reason.

The sea? We're near the sea?

Kath was standing beside the caravan, buttoning up a calico dress. Her hair was wet, her legs and feet sandy. 'Hullo,' she smiled. 'Thought you were never going to wake up.'

'Where are we?' he asked, perplexed.

She shrugged. 'Just an overnight stopover.'

That doesn't tell me much, Trevor thought and then added, 'Where's Dad?'

'Down at the beach.'

'The beach?'

Kath smiled again, faintly, and shook the wet hair free of her face. 'Go on down, Trev. The water's really nice, not cold at all.'

He thought about that for a moment and then jumped back into the Kombi to change into a pair of swimmers.

'There's a path just over here,' Kath called after him.

He found it at the fringe of bush, a track of sandy soil, punctuated by patches of rocky ground and tree roots that arched above the soil. The rocks and tree roots made it an obstacle course of sorts, and he alternated between sprint-ing, hopping and treading carefully around things he could have stubbed his toe on or tripped over. Behind him in the distance, Kath was singing one of her songs.

The evenness of the sandy soil was marked with foot-prints – Buckley's and Kath's, he guessed. It seemed to take a long time walking over ground still cold from the night, but eventually he came within sight of the ocean's horizon, the sea blindingly reflecting the sunlight. There was the sound too, the roar of the ocean that grew increasingly louder as he walked on through the bush. And when he stopped to listen, it seemed to be all he could hear.

The trees gave way to windblown shrubs, the black ground to the white sand of the coast's edge. The pathway sloped downwards then, and slowly bushland became open beach.

Here, he stopped.

For a moment, lots of thoughts ran through his mind. Images became reality and a vague set of memories were suddenly mirrored in what now confronted him. *It can't be the same place*, he reasoned then. But the beach commanded his attention by its vastness and raw beauty, and he gave up thinking.

The sand was warm under his feet, and squeaked when he ran across it. His toes sank deep with each step into the grainy softness, until he stopped once more to look around.

To either side of him the beach stretched, a white barrier between the ocean and the green of the mainland. Peninsulas rose distantly to end this picture, headlands of faraway places. Along this length, the waves rose and foamed on to the beach. Barely within earshot, seagulls hovered and screeched. There seemed to be no one in sight.

But there was someone in the water. Someone sitting on a surfboard, motionless on a stretch of flat, still water a long way from the shore.

Trevor wandered down to the water's edge, watching.

Further out to sea a wave formed, grew, came closer and closer. The surfer was on his knees now, paddling the board along and the wave advanced, lifted him up and swept him along.

The movement was hypnotic. The surfer rose to the top of the wave. With a single deft movement he swung the board at right angles down into the wave's arc, and cut across the water amid a shower of salt spray. He repeated the movement again and again, swinging the surfboard to the left and then to the right, keeping swift pace with the wave as it crashed and hurled itself towards the shore. Every movement seemed graceful and precise and eventually ended when the wave hit the shallow water and flattened out. The surfer slid off his board and waded into the shore.

For a second, the sun had shone into Trevor's eyes and he couldn't focus or see properly, but he knew it had to be Buckley. But it was an oddly different Buckley who was carrying the old surfboard and grinning from ear to ear.

Trevor at first couldn't identify the difference exactly, but when his dad walked up to him, he could see at once what had changed.

The beard had gone. The curled ginger beard had been shaved off, and there was Buckley's face, all of it. Not the face Trevor might have imagined but an oddly young face, thin and serious.

'You look strange, Dad.'

Buckley laid the dripping board on the sand. His wet hair was streaming seawater down his face and he swept his hands across his forehead to divert the salt water from his eyes.

'Why did you shave your beard off?'

Buckley just smiled. 'A change is as good as a holiday, eh?'

'You were surfing really well.'

There was no reply.

'When I was little, I remember you surfing.'

The two of them stood there then, watching the waves form, rise and fall crashing into the shallows. Some waves became nothing, merely lumps in the water that refused to break and ended up as feeble washes of water and froth at Trevor's feet.

'You remember that?' Buckley said at last. 'When I used to surf? Years ago?'

'Mmm.'

'You seem to remember lots of things, Trev. At least that's the impression I get.'

'I guess so.' It was hard getting used to talking to that face. It was an awkward nakedness, those cheeks and chin without the security and familiarity of the beard. Trevor decided he didn't like it. 'Grow your beard back,' he said.

'I will be,' Buckley replied. 'This was only an experiment.' And he added with deliberation, 'I wanted to remember what I looked like once.'

He looked away then, and seemed to be deep in thought about something. When he spoke again, it was to say, 'Would you like to have a go on the board, Trev?'

Trevor's mouth dropped open. 'I can't swim too well, you know.'

'I'll be out there with you,' Buckley replied. 'Do you want to?'

Trevor waited a moment before nodding a reply. 'Okay.'

The water at first was a numbing coldness around his body and he hesitated before getting himself completely wet.

'Come on!' Buckley was in the water beside him. 'If you don't get your head wet, I'll give you a ducking.'

Trevor sighed and pulled a face, then clamped his nose with his fingers and sank into the water. A wave washed over him and he rose up once more, sleek and wet.

'That's better,' said Buckley. 'Now. Get on to the board and I'll take you out a bit further.'

Together, they moved out into the deeper water, rising and falling with each shore-bound wave. Trevor lay stomach-down on the board, the rough, waxed surface rubbing against his skin. He felt raw excitement and appre-

149

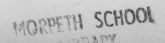

hension all at once as each wave that washed against the board threatened to throw him into the awesome depths beneath.

At last, Buckley stopped, turning Trevor and the surfboard around so that they faced the beach.

'Now what?' Trevor asked.

'We wait for a wave.'

For a while then there was a stillness around them, as the surf flattened out and rippled uselessly about. Small waves rose and fell beneath the board, lacking the power that Trevor was poised for.

The beach seemed far away at first too, but when a familiar figure in a calico dress appeared on the sand at the water's edge, Trevor realized that it wasn't that distant.

'You've got an audience,' said Buckley, waving to Kath. She waved back and folded her arms, waiting.

'Don't forget,' Buckley was saying, 'once you're with the wave, get on to your knees. Keep to the centre, and don't try standing up, not this time anyway. Just keep your balance and steer the thing much like you would a skateboard.'

Again, they waited. Trevor lay on the surfboard; beside him, Buckley trod water.

'Right,' Buckley said suddenly. 'Here you go –' and gave the board a push.

Trevor felt the wave abruptly lifting him, felt the board being forced forward. Behind him, Buckley yelled, 'Paddle!'

He paddled frantically, and the board kept pace with the heightening wave.

'Kneel!' Buckley yelled.

Shakily, Trevor eased on to his knees and for a brief moment felt himself actually steering the plank of fibreglass, felt himself in control. He plunged headlong down a slippery dip of salt water, and with an effort steadied the board's course. The balance seemed right, and he straightened up a little. In a single swift movement, the wave threw him off the board into the water.

For a moment, he was churned madly about before struggling to his feet in chest-deep water. There was a roar as another wave broke over him and churned him under once again, flooding his mouth and nose with water. He finally struggled upright in the shallows near the shore, trying to catch his breath. The board had been washed up on to the sand beside him.

'Are you all right?' said Kath.

Trevor spluttered and coughed. At that very moment he felt far from all right, but managed to answer 'yes', nevertheless. He started coughing again, then, and Kath obligingly slapped his back.

'That was classic, Trev,' she said. 'The first few moments, you very nearly had it. If you –'

'I lost my balance,' he spluttered. 'That bloody wave was all over me.'

Buckley emerged from the surf. 'Not bad, not bad. Your first try on a board and all. You'll have to practise if you want to improve.'

'Can I practise now?' Trevor's voice dropped off as Buckley shook his head in reply.

'Not right now. You'll have another chance to, soon enough . . .'

'When?'

'. . . but right now, we have to get on the road.'

The waves crashed and spilled on to the sand. The sea's presence was demanding and warmly hypnotic. For a few quiet moments, the three of them watched the ocean, before turning to leave. It was afternoon, and they were driving.

The sun was hot on his legs, because he was on the Kombi's front seat, wedged between Kath, who was driving, and Buckley, who was gazing through the open passenger window. In his ears were the familiar Kombi noises, the bangs and rattles, the cough-splutter of the engine that changed pitch with each change of gears.

They were on a road that twisted and wound its way through hills and lush valleys, over creeks and rivers and through small towns with nothing but the highway to define them. Electrifying this landscape was the occasional glimpse of the nearby coastline and a width of ocean.

They were moving again.

In his mind, he could picture a school he'd been to. He could see a barren classroom and the children who occupied it, he could see trees, playground and orderly morning assemblies. Abruptly, his mind pictured a person called Fuller, and he thought then about his mother buying him football clothes and about training sessions and football matches.

He thought about Martin Grace then, but it was only a faint sort of image, because he still didn't fully understand Martin. And then, he thought about himself and his parents.

He opened his eyes.

The breeze swept in through the Kombi's open window, and Kath's long light hair blew with it. She was humming familiar tunes and although she was busy driving, Trevor sensed from the distant expression on her face that her thoughts were very much elsewhere. Buckley, meanwhile, was still gazing through the window at the passing landscape, a faint smile crossing his stubbly face.

Trevor smiled too, and a cluster of sadnesses seemed to leave him. Images of the town, the caravan park, Martin Grace, Fuller and the team were suddenly shrivelled, insignificant memories. An inexplicable optimism swept through him, and he tried to think of what was happening right now. This time, something seemed abundantly different, yet he was at odds explaining to himself the exact difference. Finally, he gave in.

'Where are we going?' he asked.

'Hmmm?' Buckley seemingly hadn't heard.

'Where are we going?' Trevor repeated. 'Now?'

Buckley seemed to think for a while then, as he tried to frame an adequate reply. The Kombi drove on, the incessant engine noise matched calmly by the song Kath was still humming. Fleetingly, Trevor's mind filled with vague pictures of a time long past. For a moment, he could see himself as a small child again, four years old in a place he had never really forgotten . . .

Buckley smiled then, and at last replied.

'We're going home, Trevor.'

ABOUT THE AUTHOR

Simon French wrote his first novel, *Hey Phantom Singlet*, when he was still at school. It was published in 1975 when he was seventeen, to wide critical acclaim, and a paperback edition was produced two years later. He worked on his second book, *Cannily, Cannily*, during a three-year sojourn in Bathurst, New South Wales, where he was on a teacher training course. After a year's teaching in a small country town, he is now an infants' teacher in Sydney's outer western suburbs. He enjoys listening to music, playing the guitar, painting, and exploring the country.

GOODNIGHT MISTER TOM
Michelle Magorian

The year is 1939. Britain is on the brink of World War II and London's East End children are being evacuated to the country. At first Willie Beech is disturbed by the peace and quiet and terrified of the animals he encounters, but gradually, living with old Tom Oakley, he is accepted and loved for the first time in his life. But then his happiness is rudely shattered by a summons from his mother ...

GOODBYE, CHICKEN LITTLE
Betsy Byars

Jimmie Little's family were always doing reckless things that terrified and embarrassed him. He tried to avoid getting involved – dubbing himself Chicken Little in an effort to joke away his fear. And now Uncle Peter had bet that he could walk across the thin layer of ice covering the swift and merciless depths of the Monday River, which had never been done before. The foolish and dangerous stunt has tragic results, leaving Jimmie with an overwhelming sense of responsibility. How he handles his guilt makes this at once a moving yet occasionally funny book, which will appeal to readers of 10 or more.

TRAVELLER

Anne de Roo

In the pioneering days of the 1850s, sixteen-year-old Tom Farrell sets sail for New Zealand and a job on a sheep station. After the gruelling sea voyage, Tom anticipates his new life with eagerness – but worse is to come. The journey to the sheep station involves crossing miles of trackless plain, and Tom becomes separated from his guide ... Thanks to a weak and starving sheepdog named Traveller, Tom is finally saved, and as this remarkable dog's history is unfolded, some very strange things come to light.

THE COURAGE OF ANDY ROBSON

Frederick Grice

Transplanted far north to stay with his aunt and uncle following his father's terrible accident in the mine, Andy felt lost and lonely in the quietness of the country. His Uncle Adam was Park Warden to Lord Hetherington's estate and responsible for the wellbeing of the famous wild white cattle of Lilburn; Lord Hetherington's rude and un-caring attitude did not make his work any easier, since he regarded the cattle as an expensive nuisance and Uncle Adam's requests mere irritations. Then disaster struck, not just once but twice, and Andy found himself forced to draw on reserves of strength and courage that he hadn't realized he possessed.

Heard about the Puffin Club?

... it's a way of finding out more about Puffin books and authors, of winning prizes (in competitions), sharing jokes, a secret code, and perhaps seeing your name in print! When you join you get a copy of our magazine, *Puffin Post*, sent to you four times a year, a badge and a membership book.

For details of subscription and an application form, send a stamped addressed envelope to:

The Puffin Club Dept A
Penguin Books Limited
Bath Road
Harmondsworth
Middlesex UB7 0DA

and if you live in Australia, please write to:

The Australian Puffin Club
Penguin Books Australia Limited
P.O. Box 257
Ringwood
Victoria 3134